# THE
# COURAGE
# TO
# STAND

# RUSSELL MOORE

# THE
# COURAGE
# TO
# STAND

### FACING YOUR FEAR
### WITHOUT LOSING YOUR SOUL

B&H
PUBLISHING
NASHVILLE, TENNESSEE

Published by B&H Publishing Group
Nashville, Tennessee

Dewey Decimal Classification: 179
Subject Heading: COURAGE / CHRISTIAN LIFE / FEAR

Cover design and illustration by Stephen Crotts.

1 2 3 4 5 6 7 • 24 23 22 21 20

*To my parents,*
*Gary and Renee Moore,*

*Thank you.*

# Contents

# Introduction

Whenever I lose my way in life, there are two maps on the wall that can help me navigate my way back home. That happens more often than I would like to admit, but whenever it does, the maps are always there. One of those maps is of the state of Mississippi, with a dot hovering over the coastline there where I grew up. The other map is of a land called Narnia. Those maps help remind me who I am, but, more importantly they remind me what I'm not, what I almost was.

And what I almost was is a teenage suicide.

That last sentence there I have written, and unwritten, at least a dozen times. I'm scared to disclose it, because I've never discussed it before, even with close friends. But that's what this book is about: finding a way in the midst of fear, to somehow, having done all else, to stand.

Those maps are just scraps of paper, but, to me, they are almost portals to alternative realities, and in one of those realities I am dead. In the other reality, I found my way here, through a wardrobe in a spare room somewhere in England.

Many people, I know, spend a lifetime traumatized and scarred by their childhood religious community. I've heard the stories so often that it startles me how similar the narratives can be, no matter how different the religious backgrounds. Most of the skeptical unbelievers I meet on college campuses or elsewhere are civil and sincere, but when I encounter someone who is hostile or ridiculing of me because of my faith, I've learned to see that, in almost every case, there's a great deal of pain underneath, pain that comes often from some cruel or disappointing religion. That, though, is not my story. As a matter of fact, my home church growing up was a respite for me, the safest place I could, or can, imagine. Our pastors were, for the most part, authentic and humble leaders, and, even now, I aspire on my best days to be like them. The men and women in that church were like that too. Flawed and fallen, as we all are, they modeled for this child a world in which the gospel really did seem to be good news. And when they sang, "I'm so glad I'm a part of the family of God," I could tell they really meant it. And so did I. I don't wish to idealize that little congregation, but it's hard not to do so when, the older I get, the more I am convinced that God really was at work in that place. I well up with gratitude whenever I smell anything that evokes one of those musty Sunday school rooms, or whenever I taste cinnamon gum, which one of the elderly ladies would hand me right before church. When I recite the creedal phrase "I believe in the communion of saints," what first comes to mind is not an assembly of ancient church fathers or reformers or famous missionaries, but these people— truck drivers and cafeteria workers and electricians, who showed me what it meant that Jesus loved me.

Moreover, our liturgical calendar was low-church, and rooted in Nashville rather than Rome or Canterbury, but the rhythms of that calendar ordered my life just as surely as for a medieval monk, with fall and spring revivals, summer youth camps, weekly Sunday schools and evangelism training and choir practices. And, of course, there was the Bible. Sometimes I feel that modern English is my second language, with King James my native tongue. I lived and breathed and found my being in that book, and I have the award ribbons to prove it. Hard to imagine anything like this now, but in that world "Sword Drills" were common, sort of like a spelling bee except in which children compete to find Bible verses the fastest ("sword" because the Word of God is the "sword of the Spirit" and is "sharper than any two-edged sword"). More often than not, I won those duels, not because I was smarter or holier than my peers, but because I was transfixed with the stories of that book. That was true even in those parts of the Bible I found incomprehensible, such as, up until puberty, the Song of Solomon, and, up until now, the Revelation of John.

My church was not a place of trauma, but, nonetheless, trauma found me. Around the age of fifteen I found myself in a dark wood, a spiritual crisis that spun out into a nearly paralyzing depression. While my church didn't prompt this crisis, I couldn't turn to the church at that moment because I started to wonder if Jesus was the problem, not the solution. What prompted the crisis was the Christian world outside of my church, the American Christianity of the Bible Belt, which was easy to see because that sort of cultural religiosity was the ecosystem in which we lived. Much of it seemed increasingly to me to be buffoonish and even predatory. But, beyond all that, I started to fear that maybe Christianity was a means to an end. Again, I didn't question the authenticity of my church mothers and fathers, but I started to fear that maybe they were the exception rather than the rule to what it meant to be Christian. Though I never doubted their sincerity, I started to wonder if maybe they, along with me, were being duped.

Some of that had to do with the explosion at the time of prophecy conferences and end-times expos, in nearly every town and almost everywhere across the airwaves. People who would rarely even go to church, any church, would drive miles to hear an evangelist explain why the founding of the secular state of Israel meant that, almost guaranteed, the world would end by 1988. That was when I turned sixteen. That was supposed to be exciting to me, I knew, but I was an awkward adolescent virgin, wondering why, if I had to live firsthand through one of those incomprehensible books, it couldn't be the Song of Solomon instead of the Revelation of John.

The year 1988 came and went, of course, with my prophecy charts and my virginity both still firmly within my possession. But no one apologized or even explained why those predictions didn't happen. Likewise, the Soviet Union was supposed to be the Gog and Magog of Bible prophecy, setting off the cataclysmic Battle of Armageddon, we were told. Eventually, though, the flag would come down from the Kremlin, with no one to tell us why the world was never forced to kneel before Gog. The problem, for me, was not just the obvious failures of accuracy here, contrasted to the authority with which such predictions were made; it was that the biblical proofs of all this stuff seemed secondary to what sort of interest they would draw. The Bible verses used to support all of these provocative claims were peppered about so quickly, with no context, that one would have to be a Sword Drill champion even to find them all, much less to fact-check the claims. But a Sword Drill champion is what I was. And it started to seem that the point of all of this was something other than a careful reading of what the Bible said.

So what could the point be? Maybe it was politics or culture. Politicians showed up in churches around the region, though not in ours, and I could see that these "testimonies" almost always happened right around election time, and the politicians were all up for re-election, and held similar partisan affiliations as the preachers who invited them. If Jesus could call both tax collectors *and* zealots in the first century, I wondered why all of his followers, or at least those who were able to share their stories from the pulpit, were of just one stripe now. Tax collectors, of course, were not the equivalent of Internal Revenue Service employees in our own time, but were instead collaborators with the Roman Empire, often defrauding and intimidating their own people in so doing. The zealots were those who wanted, by any means necessary, to uproot the Roman occupying forces. No two groups could have had a wider social and cultural divide, and that was a model I did not see in the culture around me. Though this sort of partisan Christianity was mercifully rare in my own church, everywhere around me, it seemed almost schizophrenic on the relationship of the church to the state.

When it had to do with issues popular with the "base" of churchgoers in the area—even issues as tangential as tax-cuts or spending levels for weapons systems—there was a clearly "Christian" position, and we should, of course, stand up for Jesus on those things, because he is Lord of all, or not lord at all. But when it came to, say, the way we treat black people— which one might think was an important question for post-Jim Crow Mississippi—suddenly an impenetrable separation of church and state was erected that would make even Thomas

Jefferson blush. In those cases, suddenly, we were to see that this was a "sin problem, not a skin problem" and that just getting people saved would cause this to correct itself. I wasn't exactly sure how, since personal salvation didn't automatically produce sexual morality, without discipleship. But apparently this could. Family values had to be talked about, and so did all sorts of other issues.

But not race.

And not issues less popular with those doing the preaching or with those making decisions about whether the pastor would still be paid for preaching. Those issues were "distractions," despite all the Bible said about love of neighbor and just treatment of the vulnerable. For much of the Bible Belt of that time, there would be no such distractions, and thus plenty of time to discuss whether supermarket scanners were a test run for the Mark of the Beast.

The pastors that led our church, with very rare exceptions, were those who were, no matter whether people liked them or not, "above reproach" morally and ethically. But I could see all sorts of sordid behavior in the Christianized culture around us. Whenever a person on the "other side" of the culture wars was caught in a sexual scandal, Christians would say that that's where secularism leads. But when a preacher was discovered to be fondling a child, he was suddenly and quietly "called by God" to another church. That twinkling-of-an-eye Rapture didn't happen to us, but it did to lots of preachers, who were moved on along to prey on a new unsuspecting pasture. I saw elsewhere in the Christian world, among Christians who thought that our church didn't "preach hard enough against sin," an adult washing a child's mouth out with soap because the child said "Gosh darn it!" (a euphemism, it was explained, for taking the Lord's name in vain). But no one washed out the mouths of those Christian leaders, including pastors who used racist epithets and trafficked in racist jokes.

No one seemed to notice when the Christian man, who talked about little other than "traditional family values," would beat his four-year-old daughter with a belt strap when he saw her skipping along with her friends and concluded she was "dancing." Now, thirty-some years later, I can still see the infernal rage in his eyes, as he catechized his daughter against dancing with each word in rhythm with the pelting of that strap against her skin. And, were you to put me in an extemporaneous Sword Drill, I could find for you in seconds the proverb such men would use to justify their tantrums, should anyone ever have bothered to question them. My church was a refuge of life, but, beyond its walls, the Bible Belt often seemed more belt than Bible.

For me, these questions were not just about seeking out the truth. They were an existential threat. If Christianity were just a means to an end, if Jesus were just a hood ornament on top of southern honor culture, then that means that what held everything in the cosmos together was not the Sermon on the Mount but the survival of the fittest. All that would be left is a universe red in tooth and claw, a universe that at its heart is not about love but about power. If that were so, then, however well-intentioned the people were who taught me to sing it, Jesus didn't love me, no matter how the Bible told us so. I wanted to die—and I realize only now that my life as a writer started not with my writing short stories or essays but suicide notes, trying to explain why I didn't want to hurt anyone but that I couldn't bear to live.

# Chapter One

# Courage and Crisis

## *What Are You Doing Here?*

A long with the Mississippi map, another hangs on my wall. And because it hangs here, I did not hang there.

The reason for all this was because I happened to look, at just the right moment, at a shelf in a bookstore where I saw the name "C. S. Lewis," and wondered why it was familiar to me. Quickly I recalled the name as the author of *The Chronicles of Narnia*, all of which I had read as a child, multiple times over. To me, these were more than just books of my childhood. "The weird thing about the Narnia books for me was that mostly they seemed true," wrote novelist Neil Gaiman. "These were reports from a real place."[1] That was certainly true for me. Until I was older than I would like to admit, I would feel to the back of wardrobes to make sure there wasn't a snowy landscape back there, complete with a faun and a lamppost. Narnia seemed like a real place, even when the world around me seemed false, when I was, though still a Christian, like the kind of Christian who, in the words of Walker Percy, "lost faith in everything but the Fall of Man."[2] My adolescent depression meant that, for several months, I was pinned to my own kind of Stone Table, but, too small to attract my notice, there were mice nibbling at the ropes that held me there. And Aslan was on the move.

The book I saw on the shelf was *Mere Christianity*. Out of familiarity with Lewis, I gave it a chance, and I was surprised by (what I came eventually to see was) joy. The reason I loved the Narnia books was because Lewis didn't write to me as to a child, but as a fellow pilgrim. This book was the same. I didn't need his apologetic arguments for the existence of God, and the deity of Christ, and so on. I already believed all of that. What reached me was the fact that, in some way I can't quite describe, I could tell that he was not trying to sell me something. He was bearing witness to something true, to Someone who was Truth.

In that sense, just when I needed him, Lewis was a kind of prophet. He was not a prophet, of course, in the sense of some direct revelation from God, and he would be the last to claim such, which is one of the reasons I listened to him. He was a prophet in the sense that, when I suspected I was being lied to, he told me the truth. And, in that, he was almost in the spirit of the prophet Elijah. By that, I mean he seemed to come out of nowhere, with a kind of Radio Free Bible Belt from beyond the grave.

Like Elijah in his garment of hair, Lewis would even have looked bizarre in my culture, with that Oxford cloak, pipe hanging from his mouth, and a sardonic look as if to say that he might well play cards and dance, all the while daring some Baptist to take a belt to him. More than that, though, he made sense. Like Elijah and the prophets in his line, all the way down to John the Baptist, Lewis seemed to converge along with them at that scene of the Jordan River painted at the back of the baptistery in my home church. And with that community of prophets, he pointed away from himself to say, "Behold, the Lamb of God."

Not all at once, but gradually, the snow of that winter in my psyche started to melt, and my Screwtape terror brightened into a Narnian reality. Lewis showed me the big vista of the church through the ages, with all of its fumbling and sinning and loving and serving, and sent me right back to what I had learned from my home church. There were frauds and hucksters out there, indeed, but Jesus was alive, and my church pointed in the right direction. Lewis took me there and back again, the long way around.

My adolescent spiritual crisis is hardly that important to the world. Most faiths that persist are tested and tried along the way. But, over the years, I've come to see that many have lived through the same sort of crisis, and not all of them ended up where I did. A few years later, I was startled with familiarity as I read about a similar teenage crisis experienced by the author James Baldwin. What I noticed was that Baldwin, like me, didn't come to that crisis by way of the intellect, as though doubting the credulity of the supernatural. That came later. For him, as for me, what he felt was fear. He started to see some people, including part of himself, for whom the gospel was just a "gimmick," a way to survive the toughness of the world, and he started to wonder if that's all there is to it. He had supposed, he wrote, "that God and safety were synonymous," and so: "I became, during my fourteenth year, for the first time in my life, afraid—afraid of the evil within me and afraid of the evil without."[3] Baldwin was, by the time he wrote those words, an atheist. If he had attacked Christianity with anti-supernatural ridicule, I could have rebutted him. If he had presented himself as morally superior to the church, I could have seen through that. But he didn't seem smug or proud or even cynical. He seemed crushed, just like I had been. "I was even lonelier and more vulnerable than I had been before," he wrote. "And the blood of the Lamb had not cleansed me in any way whatever."[4]

What I had experienced, however, was not a crisis of faith, but a crisis of courage. I was afraid. I was afraid that the horrors I saw among the born-again meant that there was no new birth, that there was no hope, no point, no meaning, and, beyond all of it, no home at the end of it all. I would be a cosmic orphan, thrown into a chaotic universe with no eye on the sparrow, and no eye on me. And the ultimate outcome of all that would be doom. When I started to lose my religion, I panicked because I realized that would mean losing Jesus, losing myself, losing my future, and losing that church, those people who never even knew I was in trouble, but loved me through it anyway. So, after nearly falling into an abyss, I stood back up, and I am still standing.

My crisis came to a head when, walking near my house under the stars, I turned over my fears, my doubts, my future, to Jesus. Something changed that night, but I wish I could tell you that what that night meant was the end of my crisis, the full transition to courage from cowardice. I want to recall that night as if it were the account of Fyodor Dostoevsky's Alyosha Karamazov who also fell to the ground under a starry sky, who also watered the earth with his tears. "But with each moment he felt clearly and almost tangibly something as firm and immovable as this heavenly vault descend into his soul," Dostoevsky wrote. "Some sort of idea, as it were, was coming to reign in his mind—now and for the whole of his life and unto ages of ages. He fell to the earth a weak youth and rose up a fighter, steadfast for the rest of his life."[5] But that's not my story.

I stood up, yes, but I can hardly say that I have been a steadfast fighter for the rest of my life. As a matter of fact, I am most often still that weak youth of thirty years ago. That crisis so long ago prepared me for every crisis since. I'm not surprised now when I see Jesus used as a mascot to prop up some identity politics or power agenda, or even to cover up private immorality or public injustice. I'm angrier than ever when I see that, because I know what is happening to the overlooking fifteen-year-olds like me. But I know Jesus well enough now to see that such is not about him at all. That doesn't mean, though, that I am any less scared. And I often find myself, just as then, frustrated that I cannot live up to the Bible stories embedded in my conscience. What I want to be is the kind of Christian who is willing to stand for Jesus, to be willing to stand alone if necessary. But, more than that, I want to be the kind of Christian who can stand that way without the fear of being out of step with whatever group of people I am looking to for approval.

That spiritual crisis ended, and my faith was steeled, more resilient than it had been before. But that same problem—the pull toward fear, especially what the Bible calls "fear of man"—lingers in me, and I would wager in some way or the other in you. I often need an Elijah to appear—out of nowhere—to point me in the right direction. So, like a Passover meal in my psyche, I keep an empty chair there for Elijah.

And yet, I've noticed that when I am the most scared, Elijah is the last person I want to see. During a dark moment in my life, I noticed that, without any conscious decision on my part, I altered my daily Bible reading of the Old Testament, just ever so slightly. At the time I had been reading through 1 and 2 Samuel, and then on into 1 Kings through the life of Solomon, and then suddenly veered on over to the Psalms. I noticed that, and questioned why. As I thought about it I became convinced that subconsciously I was avoiding that middle section of 1 and 2 Kings because I knew who was there: a prophet called Elijah. I wanted to avoid him the same way a laid-off person wants to avoid her "Employee-of-the-Month" neighbor, or the way an obese person wants to avoid his marathon-running brother-in-law. And the reason is the comparison only highlights one's inadequacies, whether real or perceived. Once again, I was crushed and fearful and cowardly, not the fiery Elijah I had wanted to be.

At first glance, that makes sense. When we think of Elijah, we think of steely determination, the willingness to defy gods and kings, in scorn of the consequences. If you asked me as a child in Sunday school to draw a picture of Elijah, I would have drawn the scene that I thought summed up the prophet's life, when he stood on Mount Carmel, and called down fire from heaven. If you're not familiar with the account, it is really about a kind of contest between the prophet and the priests of the Canaanite deity Baal. After pronouncing judgment on the erring king of Israel, Ahab, for his efforts to merge the worship of Israel's God with these fertility idols, Elijah subpoenaed all of the other side's religion-mongers to pray to their respective gods, to see who would answer with fire.

In that moment, Elijah is everything I want to be. He verbally spars with his opponents—sarcastically mocking their impotent god. He confidently pours water on his own sacrifice, cries out to the skies, and then, with a bolt of incandescence, the fire falls. That is strong; that is "prophetic." That's what it means to stand, I tend to think to myself. So, in those moments, I just want to do an end-run around that hair-suited seer.

But that's harder to do than it may appear. Try to avoid Elijah in moving through the Bible and one will find, much as King Ahab and Queen Jezebel did, that he has the annoying habit of showing up persistently, often when he is least expected. That's somewhat surprising because, at least in terms of space devoted to him, Elijah is not a major figure in the biblical account. As a matter of fact, he is a kind of mayfly in the sunset of the Scriptures; one moment we see him and the next he is gone, in a literal blaze of glory. But Elijah's absence is felt all over the rest of the Bible, even as his mantle and his spirit move on through the line of prophets. Indeed, the very last words of the Old Testament canon are about Elijah, and they are about the future, not the past. God said through the prophet Malachi: "Behold, I will send you Elijah the prophet before the great and awesome day of the LORD comes" (Mal. 4:5). And then there's silence, for four hundred years.

When the biblical story resumes in the New Testament, Elijah is everywhere present, in hints and allusions and images. John the Baptist carried out the motif of the wild man of the woods with a word of impending judgment. And Jesus identified this baptizer—his own cousin—with the prophecies of the return of Elijah. At the same time, in his inaugural explanation of what his ministry would be, Jesus pointed to the ministry of Elijah and his successor Elisha as demonstrating that the good news of God's kingdom was always meant to overwhelm national and ethnic boundaries (Luke 4:25–27). And, in the Gospels, many of the aspects of Jesus' calling evoke scenes from the life of Elijah—from the raising of a widow's son from death to miraculous provision of food to a visible ascent into heaven.

Moreover, many scholars have noticed a similar Elijah theme in the life of the apostle Paul, especially in his recounting of his story in the opening chapters of the letter to the Galatians. Saul of Tarsus, after all, thought himself to be operating out of "zeal"—the very word used of Elijah in his mission to uproot Baalism—when he sought to wipe out the Christian gatherings in Damascus. His zeal, like that of Elijah, though in a distinct way, led to a crisis when on the road to Syria, he was confronted by the resurrected Messiah. And then Paul followed the same path Elijah did, when he thought his life's mission in jeopardy—he headed out into the wilderness, through the Arabian desert toward the place where God had met with his people at Sinai. And there, like Elijah, he experienced the presence of God in such a way that Paul was freed from the need for the approval of others, whether of credentialed apostles in Jerusalem (Gal. 2:1–10) or of the crowds of his constituency (Gal. 2:11–12). After this crisis, Paul could write, "For am I now seeking the approval of man, or of God? Or am I trying to please man? If I were still trying to please man, I would not be a servant of Christ" (Gal. 1:10).

On this theme, New Testament scholar N. T. Wright notes the connections, especially in Galatians, of the apostle Paul with the prophet Elijah. "The parallel with Elijah—the verbal echoes are so close and the reflection on 'zeal' so exact, that Paul must have intended them—indicates that, like Elijah, Paul made a pilgrimage to Mt. Sinai in order to go back to the place where the covenant was ratified," argues Wright. "He wanted to go and present himself before the One God, to explain that he has been 'exceedingly zealous,' but that his vision, his entire worldview, had been turned on its head. And he received his instructions: 'Go back and announce the new king.'"[6] One need not agree with all of Wright's conclusions to see that the tracking between Paul and Elijah seems too close to be merely coincidence.

And this connection is deeply meaningful. The words of Paul's testimony are radical to the core, revealing to us both Christ and crisis. "I have been crucified with Christ" the apostle declares (Gal. 2:20), words intended to liberate us—from fear, from our need to belong and to conform, and from our need to find safety in the movement of the crowd. But that safety and freedom and rest come about not through willing and wanting, but through crisis, and that crisis comes through the way of Elijah.

The Elijah narrative is indeed about courage, but not in the way that I always assumed. That's because I, like many of us, often misunderstand both the definition of courage and the meaning of Elijah. Much of what I admired about Elijah is not actually the point of the story. I aspire to the sort of fearlessness that could respond right back to Ahab that the king, not the prophet, was "the troubler of Israel" (1 Kings 18:17–18). The same sort of sass and swagger seems present when Elijah threatened drought, holding back rain by his word, and when he challenged the prophets of Baal to their contest on Mount Carmel. He didn't just defeat them; he humiliated them. They screamed and cut themselves, to try to get the attention of Baal, but "there was no voice. No one answered; no one paid attention" (1 Kings 18:29). Elijah did no such theatrics. He simply called for fire, and the fire fell. He was there vindicated, uncontestably, as the one who bears real prophetic power. And then he tore down their altars, and killed them all on the spot.

That seems "prophetic" to me, bold and unflinching and visibly winning. And apparently I'm not alone, since two of the disciples of Jesus expected the same thing, right after they had seen, with Jesus on a mountain, a vision of Elijah. As they moved through Samaria, the ancestral region of the despised King Ahab so many years before, James and John were offended that the village there did not receive their message, and so they asked, "Lord, do you want us to tell fire to come down from heaven, and consume them?" (Luke 9:54). I must admit that makes sense to me. But Jesus rebuked them, and kept on walking (Luke 9:55–56). Not only would he not destroy the Samaritans with fire, though, but along the way, he would tell the now well-known story portraying a Samaritan as the obedient protagonist (Luke 10:25–37). Why did Jesus reenact so much of the Elijah story, but not this? It's because he had, Luke recounts, "set his face to go to Jerusalem" (Luke 9:51). And what was waiting in Jerusalem? Elijah knew, because, while transfigured in light on the mountain, the old prophet spoke to Jesus "of his departure, which he was about to accomplish at Jerusalem" (Luke 9:31). What was waiting in Jerusalem was the cross.

When it comes to courage, Mount Carmel is not the hinge point of the Elijah story, but a prelude to something else. Right after this moment of triumph, Jezebel—the murderous wife of Ahab—vowed to see Elijah dead by the next day. Of Elijah, the Bible states: "Then he was afraid, and he arose and ran for his life" (1 Kings 19:3). The story only goes downward from there as Elijah treks out into the wilderness to flee from this threat. Far from the flannel-graph Spartacus I have expected since Sunday school, the picture of Elijah in the wilderness is almost pathetic. He is afraid. He is weak to the point of collapse. He is lonely. He is exhausted. He is questioning his own calling and mission. He seems depressed to the point of, at best, whining and, at worst, self-harm. And, even at the resolution of the crisis, God speaks to him not of his own bright future, but of what God will do through others, rendering Elijah seemingly irrelevant.

Most often when I have heard this account taught or preached, the focus has been on Elijah facing some form of "burnout." The application is that human beings must protect ourselves from the sort of over-extension that can lead to this form of exhaustion. Often, along with this are the practical recommendations found in God's provision for Elijah—proper nutrition, adequate sleep, and time for prayer and reflection. This is immediately relevant, of course, because many people find themselves in just that place—maybe someone who is exhausted by care of small children or of an elderly parent or of a disabled spouse or someone who bound up all of his or her identity in a career only to come to midlife to find only numbness and disillusion. But what Elijah was facing in the wilderness was more than just "burnout," it seems to me, but rather something more comprehensive—a "breakdown." In the wilderness, God was doing for Elijah what Elijah had done on the mountain—removing the Baals, this time from the prophet's own heart.

That's why he's the model we need.

The way of courage, as defined by the gospel, is not the pagan virtue of steeliness and fearlessness, much less our ambient culture's picture of winning and displaying, or strength and swagger. Getting the climax point of the Elijah story right is important because, if we don't, we will follow him somewhere other than where he ultimately was led: to the crucified glory of Jesus Christ. Without this piece of the story, we will conclude that Elijah was the picture of courage we think we need and that we pretend to have. It's a picture of courage that is celebrated in everything from ancient Greek legends to modern action films to the cavalier confidence we feign in ourselves. But if one is missing a crucial piece of the story, one gets the story wrong, even if the facts that one have are completely right.

Consider if you put the emphasis of, say, Jesus' parable of the prodigal son on the son's asking for his father's inheritance, leaving his house, spending his living on partying and prostitutes, and then, after famine comes, ending up in the pig pen eating garbage. All that's true, but that's not what the story is about. Left with that, one would see the parable as just another wisdom teaching about what happens to ungrateful children or about the necessity of self-control. Only when we see the father running to his returning son, embracing him, and calling for celebration can we make sense of the rest of it. The same is true of Jesus' parable of the Good Samaritan. If all we read is the story of the man who is beaten by thieves and left on the side of the road, we might conclude that the point of the story is a cautionary tale of "watch out, or this could happen to you." But then we would not only miss the meaning of the story, we would come to precisely the same conclusion as that of the priest and Levite in the tale who avoided the beaten man, passing on to the other side of the path. Only in light of the Samaritan's mercy on this traumatized person do we see the picture of mercy Jesus was commending.

And the same is true here. We do not see in Elijah a picture of courage-through-triumph but of courage-through-crucifixion. Elijah is not, then, a "role-model" or example for us of courage. His life was a dramatic enactment, ahead of time, of the cross, just as your life is a dramatic enactment, after the fact, of that same cross.

Consider the way that Jesus identifies the "spirit of Elijah" in the life of his cousin, John the baptizer. Like Elijah, John's ministry is not all boldness and bluster. Yes, John, like Elijah, calls a rebellious people away from their idols to a living God. Yes, John, like Elijah, delivers a word of rebuke to a wicked ruler. Yes, John, like Elijah, delivers an unpopular revelation from God, in John's case that an impoverished laborer from the backwaters of Galilee is "the Lamb of God, who takes away the sins of the world." But John is no untouchable hero. Even after baptizing Jesus, and hearing the voice of God from the skies overhead pronouncing the Nazarene his beloved Son, John feared that he was wrong. From his jail cell, he sent messengers to ask Jesus, "Are you the one who is to come, or shall we look for another?" (Matt. 11:3). A narcissistic cult leader or political guru would be offended by this wobbliness, but Jesus was not. He commended John as the greatest of all the prophets up until that time. For Jesus, John's continuity with Elijah was not, as assumed, in his power and confidence, but in this weakness and fear. "From the days of John the Baptist until now the kingdom of heaven has suffered violence, and the violent take it by force," Jesus said. "For all the Prophets and the Law prophesied until John, and if you are willing to accept it, he is Elijah who is to come" (Matt. 11:12–14).

Later, after Elijah appeared on a mountain with Jesus before his disciples, Jesus said that his followers misunderstood what they should expect from Elijah. They were perplexed that, after manifesting briefly, Elijah would go away, leaving Jesus alone, and on his way to crucifixion. They asked why the teachers of the Scripture said that Elijah must return first, before the restoring of all things. Jesus did not point them to Elijah's winning argumentation, nor to his miraculous scenes, but to his humiliation and suffering. "Elijah does come first to restore all things. And how is it written of the Son of Man that he should suffer many things and be treated with contempt?" Jesus taught. "But I tell you that Elijah has come, and they did to him whatever they pleased, as it is written of him" (Mark 9:12–13).

Indeed, the Scripture presents John from start to finish as starkly vulnerable. We see him first, not thundering on the side of the riverbank, but as an embryo, leaping in the womb of his mother in the presence of his likewise in utero Lord. Even when we do find the fiery prophet we expect, he is essentially exiled from his home and community, eating an unpalatable diet and preaching an even more unpalatable message. And then, of course, we see him ultimately as a head on a silver platter. None of this is a deviation from the way of Elijah. It is the way of Elijah. That's why when Jesus identified himself with Elijah, he was right away exiled from his community and in danger of an angry hometown crowd throwing him from the precipice of the mountain overlooking his village (Luke 4:28–30).

All of that is because the "fire from heaven" Elijah is explained by the "lost in the wilderness" Elijah, not the other way around, just as the glory we have in Jesus is explained by the crucified Christ, and not the other way around. The cross is not a momentary deviation from glory, but where we find a glory that is different from that of the world, different from what we would create for ourselves. And the courage of Elijah is seen not, first of all, when he is "owning" Ahab with figurative and literal firepower, but when, it seems, Ahab is "owning" him.

At the moment of crisis and collapse, that's when he encountered God. And that's where he, and we, can find the courage to stand. But even that language of "standing" can deceive us. We talk about "standing" for what we believe, and what we mean is usually a pose of confidence, like leadership coaches who tell their clients to project strength through body language—in some cases, to literally place their hands on their hips like a superhero. But a biblical stance of glory is not that, but hands pinned down, outside of our power, as we are crucified. What it means to "stand" for Christ is not, it turns out, to evacuate our internal lives of all fear, or to humiliate our enemies with incontrovertible "winning," but instead to live out in our very lives the drama of the cross. That means that courage does not come from matching the world's power and wisdom with more of our own, but instead by being led, like Elijah, where we do not want to go (John 21:18). The courage to stand is the courage to be crucified.

That sort of courage is formed in crisis, and those crises— turning points in our lives—are sometimes hidden to us. They are usually not big moments but little, ordinary decision points that shape, over time, who we are, what we love, what we fear, and how we stand. These are the moments where things could go one way or the other, and they usually aren't dramatic and cinematic, but are more like the "butterfly effect" in time-travel stories, in which seemingly tiny movements change the future in ways you can't perceive. Courage isn't just about the cancer patient bravely facing chemotherapy, but also the healthy person who is trying to put out of her mind the lump she felt in the shower. Courage isn't just the divorced person trying to put his life back together, but the happily married couple who look at their children and wonder how they'll ever afford to send them to college. Courage isn't just the dissident refusing to deny Christ when tortured by a dictator, but the Christian in a free country who refuses to define his faith by loyalty to a politician of any sort.

That means the chief need in every era is not what we first think of when we think of courage—physical bravery, but instead what may be called "moral courage." Mark Twain once wrote, "It is curious—curious that physical courage should be so common in the world, and moral courage so rare."[7] That line is often quoted, but less often is the quote placed in context. Twain was reflecting on the ancient Roman Empire's strategy of buying the complacency of the people through trading their liberties for allowances of corn and oil. Twain saw the same factors at work in the government's pension policies for

veterans at the time. One need not agree with Twain's analogy in this case (I don't think I do) to see the larger point. He
firmly believed this, and yet Twain conceded that, for all his
opinionating about the lack of moral courage, he had failed at
this point too.

Twain was invited to make his case about those pensions
he found so odious, not before an audience of his fellow writ-
ers or journalists but before a veterans' convention, where his
viewpoint would be, to say the least, unpopular. He wouldn't
do it. "I might try to say the words but would lack the guts and
would fail," he said. "It would be one tottering moral coward
trying to rebuke a houseful of like breed—men nearly as timid
as himself but not any more so."[8] Many would agree with him
privately, Twain wrote, but they would not say so publicly, for
fear of "saying the disagreeable thing" and being out of step
with their peers. That was, he said, the sort of fear that is part
of the nature of humanity, and he didn't see it changing. This
was only a little over a century ago, and it's obvious he was right,
if not about the policy issue then about human nature. That
aspect hasn't changed yet.

Indeed, it's been a couple of millennia, since Jesus, a more
reliable authority than old Samuel Clemens, told us why moral
cowardice is so universal among human beings. Jesus did many
signs before the crowds, the apostle John wrote, and yet most
of the people did not believe. Quoting the prophetic writings,

John said, "Isaiah said these things because he saw his glory and spoke of him," and yet: "Nevertheless, many even of the authorities believed in him, but for fear of the Pharisees they did not confess it, so that they would not be put out of the synagogue; for they loved the glory that comes from man more than the glory that comes from God" (John 12:41–43).

This is hardly unique to these first-century Jewish people. Everyone, no matter whom or where or when, has similar "Pharisees"—gatekeepers of who is "in" and who is "out." Everyone fears being cast out of some sort of "synagogue." For some, it's a political tribe or a religious group or a generational cohort or just a sense of being "normal" in the world, whatever we consider to be our "world" and whatever that world considers to be "normal." We want, if not applause, then at least not rejection and insecurity. We want to find safety in the herd, and we just choose different herds. The problem is that much of what is actually defined as courage in Scripture the bridling of the passions, kindness, humility—is seen as timidity, while many who feel themselves "courageous" because they "tell it like it is" are really just seeking to be part of their protective tribes, even when those tribes are boisterous and angry. They may feel that they "stand" for something, but this is not courage, if courage is defined by Christ. To follow the way of Christ, is to stand for the things that matter, and those things are not just the right "side" on "issues" or the right "side" on "doctrines" but conformity with Christ in terms of the affections, the experiential lived reality of walking with Christ.

Courage is needed not to do radically important things, but to live out a quiet, ordinary life, with integrity and with love. That sort of life requires not just clarity about "the issues," as though our problems were with abstract issues. That sort of life requires courage, the courage to walk out there into the wilderness, not knowing where we are going, the courage to stand, and the courage to fall.

My map of Narnia is a map to nowhere, I know. Narnia is fictional, after all. But is it really? I can't help but think of how the wardrobe-pioneer Lucy wept when told she must return back home, away from Narnia and from the lion Aslan. "And how can I live, never meeting you?" she asks. Aslan assures her they will meet again prompting her brother Edmund to ask whether Aslan is there too, back in the "regular" world. "I am," said Aslan. "But there I have another name. You must learn to know me by that name. This was the very reason you were brought to Narnia, that by knowing me here for a little, you may know me better there."⁹ The map of Narnia is, in some ways, fictional, yes. But no more so than the map of Mississippi.

I've come to see that I've lived in both realities, and that Jesus was with me in both plotlines. Those experiences didn't teach me how not to fear, but they did teach me how to stand through fear, how to listen above the crowd for a voice, or maybe a roar, off there in the distance, on the other side of what's scary. No matter how confident, or anxious, you feel right now, you, like Elijah, have a calling to carry out, a pilgrimage to take. And you can find courage for the crisis, because you can find Christ in the crisis. And soon you will see that, really, every moment is a crisis.

That's not easy, though, when one cannot see what's ahead. Jesus scared his first followers, with all his talk of his impending arrest and execution and, maybe more than all that, with his talk of going away. When he saw their distress, he reminded them that his Father's house has many rooms, that he was leaving to prepare a place for them. "And you know the way to where I am going," he said (John 14:4). His disciple Thomas spoke up. We call him "doubting Thomas," quite unfairly, but what I hear in Thomas's voice is not doubt but fear. He was afraid that Jesus had disclosed a landmark and a time to meet him, or maybe a secret incantation that would open a portal to the other side. Maybe, Thomas probably wondered whether he was asleep when these instructions were given. "Lord we do not know where you are going," Thomas pleaded. "How can we know the way?" (John 14:5). Jesus said, "I am the Way" (John 14:6).

Elijah walked that Way, and so must you. Your courage will not be found in your triumphant Mount Carmel moments, when you scatter your enemies, real and imagined, from in front of you, and when you can see clearly how protected and accepted you are. Your courage will be forged instead, like that of Elijah and everyone else who has followed this path, when you cannot stand on your own at all, when you are collapsed in the wild places, maybe even begging for death. Like Elijah, you will hear the words, "What are you doing here?" Elijah thought he was walking to Mount Sinai, but he was really walking toward Mount Calvary. And so are you. Only the crucifiable self can find the courage to stand. Do not be afraid.

There is no map here. But you know the Way.

Chapter Two

# Courage and Anxiety

## *Confidence through Fear*

The doorstep of a devil-haunted church was the scariest place I ever stood. And, in some ways I've been standing there ever since. That summer I was homesick —ten years old and away for the first extended time from both my parents and the house where I had always lived. My little brother was with me, and we were visiting for a few weeks with my uncle, the pastor of a church in rural Tennessee. Despite the longing for home, my brother and I looked forward every day to chasing each other through the woods, looking for Civil War-era muskets in the fields of the once-battlefield now national park nearby. But, more than any of that, we looked forward to bedtime each night, because that's when my uncle would read us stories before lights out. I had no idea that those readings would lead me right into a horror story of my own.

For whatever reason, the stories my uncle chose to read us were almost always by Edgar Allan Poe. I've often wondered whether Jack London or Charles Dickens or Herman Melville would have made for a better option for nervous children in an unfamiliar setting, right before they were expected to go to sleep. Nonetheless, whether this reading selection was a good choice or a poor choice, night after night, a Poe choice it was. To this day, I cannot stand the sound of a beating heart or the sight of a swinging pendulum. The fiction was one thing, though; the fact something much more complicated.

That first Saturday night that we were there, my uncle finished up story-hour by pulling askew the curtains on the window and looking out at the lit-up church building next door. His tone was hushed and grave, just as it was when he was read- ing us those ghostly tales.

"Boys," he said, nodding toward the church. "Can you imagine how many demons are in that church right now?"

Internally, I started to question what sort of church my uncle led: was this a satanic cult? Why would there be demons in the house of God? He said that we should remember that we live in a world of spiritual warfare, that we wrestle, as the Bible says, not against flesh and blood but against "the rulers, against the authorities, against the cosmic powers over this present darkness" (Eph. 6:12). Because what would happen that next morning in that building was of the utmost importance—the worship of God, the proclamation of the gospel—the forces of the Devil would not like this at all, and would do anything to disrupt it. Those demons, he said, are probably filling that sanctuary right now.

And then it was lights out.

"Can you boys imagine?" Why, yes, we could; I certainly could. I could imagine scarcely anything else, as, head under the covers, my mind filled with pictures of specters bouncing around the chandeliers, cackling like poltergeists. And all that I could hear was the sound of my own tell-tale heart.

My sense of ease was recovered when the sun dawned the next morning, and the worship service was normal, almost like that at my church back home. There were no claw-marks on the hymnals, nor any unearthly slime dripping from the communion table. Things were the way they were supposed to be, and all was well. Until the next Saturday night, that is, when right after storytime, perhaps *The Cask of Amontillado* that night, my uncle said that he needed me to run an errand. My aunt was preparing a dessert for a church dinner, and had forgotten her cake plate next door in the church's fellowship hall. I stood immobilized in terror. In my family culture, one could not say "no" to an adult, and certainly not to a preacher. But I knew where that fellowship hall was, on the far side of the sanctuary, in a room back behind the pulpit and baptistery. And I knew of only one door, at the front of the building. I would have to walk through that dark sanctuary, alone, and on Saturday night, the Devil's night.

Jangling the keys in my hand, I stood at the door, and realized I didn't know where the light switches were. Not wanting to take the time to feel around for them, I just stood there for a moment, listening for the sound of demons breathing. My mind casting about, I quickly wondered whether such listening was even orthodox. Demons are spirits, I remembered, fallen angels, so technically they couldn't have respiratory systems or physical mouths. So, could one hear them breathe? What was I afraid of? As I look back on it, I really wasn't fearful of those demons—were they really there—tearing my head off of my shoulders, or teleporting me with them to a fiery hell. I was afraid instead that those demons would expose me as a fraud. I was afraid that no matter how good and responsible I was, no matter how much Bible and theology I knew, that these dark spirits would see through me, that they would say of me, "Jesus I know, and Paul I recognize, but who are you?" (Acts 19:15).

When doctrinal speculating failed to calm me down, I turned to skepticism. Maybe there were no demons in there at all. Maybe my uncle told us that the same way a neighbor back home posted a "Beware of Dog" sign to ward off robbers, when all that was within her home was her blind arthritic three-legged Chihuahua. Maybe my uncle just wanted to keep us from trespassing into the church, by telling us a horror story we had no choice but to believe. But that line of reasoning was even scarier than the demons. If my uncle were just using the supernatural to control our behavior, then could that be what people were doing with all of it—with Jesus himself? And so, I just ran for my life, in and out of the fellowship hall, past all the pews, and into the night outside. Because it took me a while to come back into the parsonage, my uncle assumed I had had trouble finding the cake plate. But that wasn't it. I was working up my courage, to pretend—to appear nonchalant and unfazed by the scariness of the trek. I wanted to project an image of maturity and strength. I was scared, yes, but, more than that, I was scared of being scared. And, even more than that, I was scared of looking scared.

If I had known how to listen to what my fear was telling me back then I would have learned something key about the meaning of the rest of my life, especially in terms of what it means to follow Jesus. The concept of Elijah in the wilderness was not one that came to mind, in that moment, although I was comparing myself to the whole gallery of my biblical heroes, wondering why I could not be as "strong and courageous" (Josh. 1:6). But if the Elijah crisis is to show us something about what courage is, we must start by asking why Elijah was in the wilderness there in the first place. That, in fact, is the question God twice asked: "What are you doing here, Elijah?" (1 Kings 19:9, 13). Both times Elijah gave a recitation of his external situation: "I have been very jealous for the LORD, the God of hosts. For the people of Israel have forsaken your covenant, thrown down your altars, and killed your prophets with the sword, and I, even I only, am left, and they seek my life, to take it away" (1 Kings 19:10, 14).

But God had already told us, the readers, why Elijah was there. When Jezebel, the foreign-born wife of the king of Israel, heard about Elijah's Mount Carmel humiliation of her and Ahab's mashed-up religion, she vowed to have him executed by the next day. The Bible states, with matter-of-fact reporting: "Then he was afraid, and he arose and ran for his life" (1 Kings 19:3). It is not likely that you will ever face a situation where a political power will make a promise to have you murdered (though, depending on where and when you live in the world, this is entirely possible), but you will face the moment, eventually if you haven't already, when you are running for your life. In order to find the meaning of courage, we must discern the meaning of fear.

One of the first arguments my wife and I had after our wedding was about how she was helping me grapple with insomnia. She would say, "Are you still awake? You really need to go to sleep; you have to be up in three hours . . ." before listing off all I had to do the next day. Now she had no concept at all of sleeplessness. As soon as she puts head to pillow, she is dreaming. And her entire family is the same way. Often at family holiday gatherings, I and the other in-laws would be the only ones awake, watching Maria, her brothers, and her parents all fast asleep, heads back and mouths open, in their chairs. I eventually explained to her that her well-meaning encouragement was actually prolonging my wakefulness, adding a level of anxiety and making the act of falling asleep even more of a task to be performed. But very few people can will themselves to sleep. By definition, sleep has to come when you are not trying to achieve it, or trying really to do anything at all.

I sometimes think that we respond to fear, at least fear in others, the way my wife did to my insomnia. Often Christians will note that perhaps the most-often repeated command in all of Scripture is "Do not be afraid," and that's true. But simply saying this does little to evaporate fear, especially if it sounds as if the one saying it is dismissing the reasons for the fear. And sure, sometimes fears are irrational and not grounded in reality. But often we are scared not because we aren't seeing what's out there in front of us but because we are.

When a magazine featured a recipe for roast suckling pig, I found myself drawn to it, mostly because of the picture of the animal on a plate with an apple in its mouth, a little more straightforward an image than what I was used to on a recipe page. But then I cringed when I read the directions: "Heat the oven to 300 degrees. Prepare the pig: Wash it under cold running water, including the cavity, and towel-dry thoroughly, the way you would dry a small child after a bath—ears, armpits, chest cavity, face, legs, backs of knees." Now, I'm no vegetarian, and I realize that carnivorous diets mean the death of something, but I cringed. Who would use the metaphor of a small child being bathed when speaking of eating a roasted pig? I said to a friend, "This sounds like Hansel and Gretel, a witch preparing a child for the oven." And, of course, at the end of that story those captured children push the witch herself into that fire. If we think about it for a moment, that story is not quite Edgar Allan Poe, but it's close, with the scariness starting from the onset, with children abandoned by their parents due to economic hardship. That's the last thing we would want to say to our children in our safe and sanitized time. We would want to shelter our children from thinking about parental abandonment, being lost in the woods, and, certainly, being captured by a carnivorous hag.

But times were not always like these. The old fairy tales and nursery rhymes were often quite similar to the scene in Hansel and Gretel—gory, violent, and scary as could be. This was because these older generations believed that children were not, in those stories, being introduced to fear, but instead were being given narratives to help them make sense of the fear they already felt. In fact, author Maurice Sendak said that his effectiveness at writing for children was precisely because his memory of what it meant to be scared prevented him from sentimentalizing the experiences of children. "I remember my own childhood vividly," he told an interviewer. "I knew terrible things. But I knew I mustn't let the adults know I knew. It would scare them."[1] While children might not know how to articulate what they fear, they intuit something that is quite true: their own fragility in a chaotic and potentially deadly world. In this case, children understand something the rest of us spend a lifetime trying to deny.

Why is it one thing to be dead and another thing to be meat? That's the question posed years ago by naturist David Quammen as he pondered why it is more disturbing to have a loved one devoured by a bear than killed in a car accident. Such a gruesome thought has never occurred to most of us, probably because our encounter with predatory animals is limited to watching them safely behind the bars of a zoo or flickering across a screen. This is because, Quammen argues, the idea of being eaten reminds us of our vulnerability in the most visceral way possible. Most human beings throughout history, until relatively recently, have had the experience of listening in the night or surveying the waters for animals that could, quite literally, eat them up. As he puts it: "Among the earliest forms of human self-awareness was the awareness of being meat."[2] We are fascinated by such creatures, whether real or mythical, and they show up often in our stories because they remind us that human beings are not always at the top of the food chain.

Quammen points out that even the Bible is obsessed with dangerous animals, beginning with the creation account of Genesis, and that it is less concerned with an abstract notion of "the environment" than with the human relationship to certain specific aspects of the creation order—such as the predatory beasts. Leviathan, the twisting serpent-dragon of the Old Testament prophets is, in his words, "the archetype of alpha predators." Moreover, heroic figures in Scripture are often pictured as slayers of dangerous animals. Think of the encounters of David and Samson with lions, for instance. This is just another way of offering the question the writer of Hebrews asked in the first century. Why, if human beings were created to rule "over every living thing that moves on the earth" (Gen. 1:28) and if all things were, in the words of the Psalmist, put "under his feet" (Ps. 8:6), do we not then see all things under our feet (Heb. 2:8)? Whether one holds to a naturalistic Darwinian view of humanity and the cosmos or to the biblical account of human dignity and uniqueness, the scene we observe often seems the same: the universe seems well-designed to kill us. And, as alpha-predators in the wild or in our imaginations remind us, we are vulnerable. The world is scary, and the flesh is weak.

Often when describing fear, psychologists or biologists will speak of a "fight or flight" mechanism at work. The idea is, of course, that when faced with a threat, creatures will respond instinctively either by taking on the threat with violence or by withdrawing from the scene of the threat. If you startle a flock of seagulls, they will usually scatter and fly away. If you startle a wolverine, by contrast, you will do well to escape with your face still attached. The concept is so popularized now that even high school students will talk in those terms when talking about human fear "triggers." Such characterizations sometimes rattle Christians because they think they deny the uniqueness of humanity. We are not, they would respond, beasts operating out of instinct, but rather those created in the image of God, with the capacity for reason and imagination. That's true, of course, but it misses the larger point: fear can often animalize us.

Fear, after all, serves a function in this fallen universe, in the same way that pain responses do. A person without the capacity for pain is not an invulnerable person but a uniquely vulnerable person, one who will not know when he is on the precipice of being killed or killing himself. In the same way, the Bible describes the "fight or flight" instinct within living creatures as a gift of God himself, as God said to Noah and his tribe: "The fear of you and the dread of you shall be upon every beast of the earth and upon every bird of the heavens, upon everything that creeps on the ground and all the fish of the sea" (Gen. 9:2).

Why? This is for the same reason park rangers will tell visitors not to feed the wildlife. A deer that loses its fear of humanity, because it sees them as a source of food, will not be able to survive in the wild. Those not alert to predators will quickly find themselves to be venison. Likewise, without a fear of falling. a human being would likely walk off of rooftops, or without a fear of fire, one might well place a hand on a hot stove.

Many of our fears are unreasoning and irrational. Looking back on our lives we can see that most of the things we worried about never came to pass. And some of our phobias are uniquely unlikely to hurt us. I once knew a woman who said her greatest fear was coconuts and, when asked why, shrugged and said that if a coconut fell from a tree it could cause head trauma. My first reaction was to just suggest that she not vacation in the tropics, but even this is rooted in something real, the fear of death, even if this manifestation of it was kind of bizarre. And that's why, when it comes to our fears, a pat "I'm sure it will be fine," or a cheery "Everything will work itself out," from a well-meaning friend usually is not comforting. We have seen enough in the world to know that everything does not, in fact, turn out fine. We fear whether we will find love. Or, if we do, whether we will be able to keep it. Will we be able to survive financially? Can we compete with whomever we believe to be our competition? Will we make our parents—if only the imaginary parents embedded in our psyches—proud of us? In those moments when we realize what we are really capable of, we fear wrecking our lives and those of the ones we love. And, of course, all of us must die. That is not all in our minds.

Poet David Whyte rightly observes that real courage is rooted in what he calls "robust vulnerability," and thus rarely feels like courage at the time. "From the inside, it can feel like confusion, only slowly do we learn what we really care about, and allow our outer life to be realigned in that gravitational pull; with maturity that robust vulnerability comes to feel like the only necessary way forward, the only real invitation, and the surest, safest ground from which to step," he writes. "On the inside we come to know who and what and how we love and what we can do to deepen that love; only from the outside and only by looking back, does it look like courage."[3]

Elijah's fearful flight into the wilderness was reasonable and rational. Jezebel did indeed have both the motive and the means to have him killed. The royal house controlled a military, an intelligence network, a system of secret police, and Elijah did not even have an informal militia with which to fight back or even a sympathetic village willing to hide him. This was not a detour from God's purposes for him, though, but rather part of those purposes. God intended for Elijah, like so many before and after him, to meet God in the wilderness.

Elijah's fear was not a lapse in his courage, but the path toward it. In fact, without fear, courage is impossible. Writing of courage in the older language of "fortitude," philosopher Josef Pieper argued: "Fortitude presupposes vulnerability; without vulnerability there is no possibility of fortitude. An angel cannot be brave, because he is not vulnerable. To be brave actually means to be able to suffer injury."[4] In other words, courage can only emerge when we can actually be harmed and we know it. That's why Elijah's fear in the wilderness is not a cautionary tale of "don't be like this," but rather an illustration of God forming courage in a servant who will need it for the days to come.

When fear is the first and the final word, the result is not courage at all. That's why the "fight or flight" analogy works so well for human beings. Now, for most people, "flight" is the easiest response to see as cowardly—the rabbit-like running away from danger. Flight, though, is not always cowardly. Jesus withdrew from the crowds when they sought to forcefully make him king (John 6:15) and from his hometown when they sought to throw him off a cliff (Luke 4:30). He often refused to engage in debates going on around him—whether in settling a family fight over an inheritance, or paying a temple tax he did not believe he owed, or plunging into some of the theological debates with the religious leaders. And other times, he engaged directly in whatever controversy was happening around him.

The sort of "flight" that is cowardly is the kind that is not directed by the Spirit but by self-preservation. This urge to protect the self is right at the nub of what it means to say that humanity is fallen. "Self-preservation has become the principle of all of life because all life is conscious (since sin) of having become subject to death; it resists death with all its strength and seeks to maintain its self, although to no avail," wrote one Dutch Christian theologian. "This is what it means to be held 'in slavery by the fear of death' (Heb. 2:15). The fear of death has become the principle of life."[5]

No matter what people assume, there is no call for Christians to participate in every argument going on around them. But there are times when stepping back from such is based not on wisdom but fear. A young African-American friend asked me once why there were no monuments for white southern pastors who spoke up for racial justice during the Jim Crow era. I replied that such monuments would be hard to build—and not because such people didn't exist (they did), but because we usually don't know their names. Pastors who spoke up on such things were summarily dismissed and often lived out their lives as cafeteria janitors or dockworkers or high school guidance counselors. That reality led many other pastors to take the warning that the same could happen to them. They would speak loudly then, "preaching hard against sin," on issues that their congregations would approve (adultery, drunkenness, disrespect of parents) and go strangely quiet when it came to an issue the Bible speaks to everywhere: how to act justly toward vulnerable, mistreated people. Many of these pastors knew better than this, but convinced themselves that they were stewarding their influence. "If I am fired, I will just be replaced by a rabid segregationist," one might conclude. "I am better off if I wait until the time is right to speak." That is, of course, the sort of cowardly response challenged by Martin Luther King Jr. in his "Letter from Birmingham Jail."

And "flight" from fear can manifest itself in ways other than obvious retreat. Notice how few comedians come from happy backgrounds. The common theme in most of their biographies is pain and bullying, with their ability to make jokes emerging as a defense mechanism to make it through a place of deep suffering. This can be good and redemptive, bringing joy out of what was pain, but it can also be a way of life, of protecting oneself. I notice often that I have the tendency toward humor whenever someone has just complimented me, or has said something meaningful and weighty. Just before writing this, a friend stood in front of me and said, "I wanted to tell you how much you have meant to me and to my family." I noticed that I deflected it within seconds with a laugh-evoking line, just to relieve the tension of that sort of authentic, intimate human moment. That's a form of cowardice.

In the same way, much of what turns out to be self-sabotaging immorality is a manifestation of cowardly flight. When I was going through an intense time of personal suffering, an acquaintance called—who had also lived through something similar—and said, "I want to plead with you not to go the way I went." When I asked what way that was, he said that he had, in the midst of his painful isolation, started using pornography, and then found himself enslaved by it. The same story has happened with drugs or alcohol or a thousand other things. For this man calling me, the issue was not so much about an excess of sexual arousal as it was escape—an escape into the "little death" of orgasm. In fact, of all the marriages I have seen collapse due to infidelity, almost none of them originated in some sort of sexual incompatibility in the marriage bed. Instead, most of them were about boredom and fear of responsibility, ultimately about fear of death. The "drama" of the affair—"does this person like me?," "How do we keep this secret?"—gave the person a nostalgic feeling of being a teenager again. That's why the apostle Paul wrote of the way of the flesh—the rule of these appetites—as a manifestation of cowardice, of a slavery to fear that ends in the grave (Rom. 8:12–13).

But "fight" can also be just as cowardly, and sometimes even more so than "flight." Again, fight, rightly defined, is a manifestation of what it means to follow God. Jesus spoke of himself as a shepherd, not in terms of his nuzzling nurture of the sheep (although carrying them and feeding them is an essential part of it), but in terms of fighting off thieves and predatory animals, as opposed to those who take flight at the first sign of danger (John 10:11–14). A certain kind of "fighting" can give the illusion of bravery. Land of Oz notwithstanding, a lion seems more "courageous" than a rabbit, not only because of its size and strength but also because of its first response to potential danger: lions do not run.

The apostle Paul warned Timothy to have nothing to do with "foolish, ignorant controversies" because they "breed quarrels," and "the Lord's servant must not be quarrelsome" (2 Tim. 2:23–25). That's because this sort of "fighting" is not about achieving anything but about protecting the quarreler—either with an image as a "fighter" or by subduing anyone who would come against him. The problem is that quarrelsome people usually think of themselves as courageous, as those who are "standing for truth" as Elijah did against Baal or Paul against the Galatian heretics. Usually, though, the sort of people who find themselves in constant quarrels would be in such quarrels no matter what religion, or no religion, they inhabit. The point for them is not to lead toward truth but, simply, to fight, which is why the controversies are often, as Paul put it, foolish and ignorant. This sort of "fighting" leads not to a more defended flock, but to a less defended one.

If everything is an existential threat, then nothing is. Quarrelsomeness may seem more like "taking action" while carrying out spiritual warfare—which is done not with frenetic activity but by spiritual means, and therefore often looks less like firing guns than like rising yeast or incubating seeds—seems like "surrender" or "passivity." But this only reflects our warped view of courage and what it really means to fight.

Notice the difference between Jesus and Simon Peter in the Gospel narratives. Based on a reading of courage as aggression and frenetic activity, Peter would seem to be courageous, and Jesus weak and timid. Peter, after all, was willing to "fight." When Jesus spoke of his impending death, Peter challenged his "weakness" and "surrender" with bluster. Peter would fight all the way to prison and even to death (Matt. 26:33–35; Mark 14:29–31; John 13:37–39). And then he did just that. As Jesus was arrested, Simon Peter drew his sword and cut off an arresting soldier's ear. But Jesus knew what was inside of all of this fervor: fear. He foretold that Peter's "fight" would disintegrate into "flight" before the rooster crowed in the morning. When Peter heard the sound of that bird, he "broke down and wept" (Mark 14:72).

But even more than just the ineffectuality of Peter's channeling of his fear was the fact that it was counter-productive to the messianic mission itself. Jesus called the bragging Simon Peter "Satan" at one point (Matt. 16:23). That's because the response resembled that of the Devil: a fear-fueled frenzy. The Devil, after all, is the one who rages "in great wrath, because he knows that his time is short" (Rev. 12:12), just like a cornered animal. Those who defeat the Devil do so not by their whirling outrage but by something that appears relatively weak by comparison: the blood of the cross and the word of their testi-monies (Rev. 12:11).

Jesus knew what the actual battle was, a battle that could only claim victory by freeing humanity from slavery to the appetites, and from the accusation of the Evil One. That took not swords-and-sorcery, but a sacrificial offering. The crowds wanted Barabbas (Luke 23:25)—a zealot and an insurgent "fighter"—because he looked strong in comparison to one who spoke in such "surrender" terms as turning the cheek to insult, and winning by losing. This is not really new, but is a tendency going back all the way to Israel turning to the firepower of Egypt to protect them (Isa. 30–31) while ignoring where the real danger lay, in a temple encroached with the graven images of false deities. Those who "fight" but who don't fight the right enemy in the right way are the equivalent of the person who, in order to vent his anger, slams his fist into a wall while his family is being murdered in the next room. Such venting of emotion may help the man to feel better about himself, but is of no help at all to the real danger afoot.

In his novel *The Moviegoer*, Walker Percy describes Binx Bolling, the suburban New Orleans stockbroker in the throes of a life crisis, going to the library when he is depressed, to read conservative and liberal controversial magazines. "Though I do not know whether I am a liberal or a conservative, I am nev-ertheless enlivened by the hatred which one bears the other,"

Bolling says. "In fact, this hatred strikes me as one of the few signs of life remaining in the world. This is another thing about the world which is upside-down: all the friendly and likable people seem dead to me; only the haters seem alive."[6] We are all living in that library now, without ever having to leave our homes. Not only that, but the quarrels are mostly about the very same thing: not about persuading opponents or making a difference in the world, but causing the quarreler to feel alive.

In reality, though, both "fight" and "flight" responses to fear are about the same thing: self-protection. The late pastor Eugene Peterson noted the difference between the different forms of skeletal systems in living things. "In the early stages of development, creatures with exoskeletons (that is, skeletons on the outside, like crabs and beetles) have all the advantages, as they are protected from disaster," he wrote. But this is not the case in the long run since, for such creatures, "there is no development because there is no memory." And yet, he noted, "Creatures with endoskeletons (that is, skeletons on the inside, like kittens and humans) are much more disadvantaged at first, being highly vulnerable to outside danger. But if they survive through tender care and protection of others, they can develop higher forms of consciousness."[7]

For Peterson, this "exoskeleton" mentality was evident in, among other things, the rich young ruler who challenged Jesus about the path to eternal life. "His material goods and moral achievements were all on the outside like a crust, and they separated him from both his neighbor and his God." Most of us are like that. We want to build a force field around us—some with our blustery, opinionated argumentativeness and some of us by burrowing down into invisibility and retreat. Either way, we are thereby acting out of instinct, to protect ourselves, rather than by walking in the way that can change us. And that change will require risk, the sort of risk we can encounter not with the resources of a crab or a beetle but with the potentiality of a baby.

And, in fact, that's exactly where fear is to lead us—toward the experience of infanthood. This is hardly imagery that conjures up courage or bravery. No sports team would claim as their mascot, "The Screaming Babies." In fact, children will make fun of one another when they are scared with taunts of "Don't be a baby!" And we can easily see why. A human baby is the classic example of an "endoskeleton"—complete with a "soft spot" on the top of the head and a neck that cannot even hold itself up. For a baby, almost everything seems terrifying. The sound of a plate falling off of a table might as well be a nuclear siren; every second with mother stepping into another room might as well be a "Hansel and Gretel" style abandonment. And all the infant can do in response to all these fears is to cry. This is exactly the point: fear is intended to lead us toward the very same desperation and sense of helplessness.

As I was writing this book, the world was plunged into a pandemic resulting in the need, for the sake of public health, for churches to stop gathering, even on Easter Sunday. This was the first Easter I had ever experienced without church. Indeed, every church I knew was empty. And, because no one knew just how bad the spread of the disease would be, something was underneath the surface of almost every Christian on this, the holiest day of the Christian calendar, and that something was fear.

At first glance, fear seems alien to Easter, belonging to Good Friday. Even our hymnody seems to reflect this. "Were You There When They Crucified My Lord?" is, in both lyric and tune, foreboding while "Up From the Grave He Arose" is so triumphant in both lyric and tune that, with different lyrics it could be a national anthem or an advertising jingle. In a sense this is right. Good Friday is meant to evoke the emotions the first disciples experienced when they thought all was lost, when even the noon skies above them turned dark. Easter is meant to evoke a new dawn, the truth that "everything sad is coming untrue."

And yet, the Gospel accounts are not so neatly categorized by emotion. The first reactions to the Resurrection were those of confusion and fear. The guards at the tomb "trembled and became like dead men," Matthew recounts, at the sight of the angel there (Matt. 28:4). That seems right enough, given that they were hired to make the tomb "as secure as you can," (Matt. 27:65) and failed. But they were not alone. The first word the angel had for the faithful women, Mary Magdalene and the other Mary, was "Do not be afraid, for I know that you seek Jesus who was crucified. He is not here, for he has risen, as he said" (Matt. 28:5–6).

These women left this announcement, the Bible says, "with fear and great joy" (Matt. 28:8), where they ran right into the resurrected Jesus. And his first words to them were, "Do not be afraid" (Matt. 28:10). As a matter of fact, the oldest documents we have of the Gospel of Mark end with the women departing the empty tomb to go tell the other disciples, with these words: "And they went out and fled from the tomb, for trembling and astonishment had seized them, and they said nothing to anyone, for they were afraid" (Mark 16:8).

One could imagine, of course, a less traumatic Resurrection, one more in keeping with the natural rhythms of winter gradually giving way to a gentle spring. But the Resurrection instead was something that, before anything else, called out fear and alarm. Why?

This is because the Resurrection is not a timeless truth about the immortality of the human being, or that "everything works out in the end." The Resurrection takes place in a graveyard, a reminder that, left to ourselves, every one of us will retreat to the dust from which we came. This is why Jesus made the point to Martha, "I am the resurrection and the life" (John 11:25). He is the only one of us who has "life in himself" (John 5:26).

The Resurrection of Jesus does indeed destroy fear, pulling us out, in fact, of slavery from the fear of death (Heb. 2:14–15). But that freedom does not come the way we usually pursue it on our own, through denial and the illusion of immortality. In order to see the glory and mystery of the Resurrection of Jesus, we must also feel the just sentence of our own deaths, the inevitability, apart from him, of our own demise. The Resurrection means that we see our lives hidden in Christ, which means that, on our own, we are the walking dead. The Resurrection of Jesus means that we follow him where he went, toward where he is. And that means, for us, Easter is not the end of the carrying of the cross but the beginning.

That's terrifying, when you think of it. And Jesus means for you to think of it. Only then can you listen to the shepherd who walks with you through the valley of the shadow of death. Only then can you know what it means to know, "Because he lives, all fear is gone."

The apostle Paul wrote that the way of "the flesh" leads to a "slavery to fear" (Rom. 8:12–15). But it is clear from his descriptions that those in this slavery probably think of themselves neither as enslaved nor as afraid. They answer the fear with their own protective resources—the pursuit of the appetites (Rom. 8:12), the appeasing of the elemental powers of this world (Gal. 4:3, 8–10), the keeping of lists of rules and regulations (Col. 2:20–23), the biting and devouring of one another in endless controversies and disputes (Gal. 5:15–25). Those who are walking by the Spirit, on the other hand, feel scared, and probably seem to be those lacking in courage, because they have given up on their internal resources or their external reassurances; they scream out in desperation "Abba! Father!" (Rom. 8:12–17).

Courage begins with an actual cry for help.

That's why Elijah was driven to the wilderness, and that's why you will be.

Elijah going out into the dark and dry places was retracing a well-worn path, one blazed by his ancestors out of Egypt, and one that would be retread again. When the Israelites were entering the land of promise, they were terrified by the ferocity of the Canaanites there. God said: "Do not be in dread or afraid of them" (Deut. 1:29). This encouragement did not come with what most of us would want. God does not build up the fact that Israel is mightier than these threats, or strong enough to fend them off. Nor does this word from God include a recounting of the glory days of Israel, or a reminder of how they had conquered bigger problems in the past and would do so again this time. No, instead, when facing fortified cities, God reminded them of when they were homeless nomads. When they were up against giants, God reminded them of when they were dependent children. "The LORD your God who goes before you will himself fight for you, just as he did for you in Egypt before your eyes, and in the wilderness, where you have seen how the LORD your God carried you, as a man carries his son, all the way that you went until you came to this place" (Deut. 1:30–31).

Elijah's fear drove him to the point of being cared for by God, almost as a child—with food to eat, with a place to sleep, with a response to his cries. That's the direction fear leads when it is leading us away from self-sufficiency and toward the gospel by which we stand. In those cases, fear is not just a reaction but a revelation.

Every year around Christmastime, someone inevitably will bring up a line from the song "It's the Most Wonderful Time of the Year." The lyric is: "There'll be parties for hosting, marshmallows for toasting; and caroling out in the snow. There'll be scary ghost stories, and tales of the glories of Christmases long, long ago." The obvious question is, "Who on earth would tell scary ghost stories at Christmas?" I once was tempted, based on that song, to pull a volume of Edgar Allan Poe off the shelf to read to my children, but, quoth my conscience, "Never, Moore." Fear and Christmas don't seem to mix. But, in fact, they do.

In the narratives of the Incarnation, fear is everywhere, but it is fear leading in two decidedly different directions. Herod, the king of Israel, was scared when he heard of the birth of the promised Son of David, because he (rightly, in the long run) saw in it the doom of his own dynasty. He was "troubled, and all Jerusalem with him" (Matt. 2:3). This fear triggered a "fight" response of the Ahab-and-Jezebel sort, namely the vow to kill all of the male children, to make sure this "troubler of Israel" never came of age. That must have seemed like strength and winning to those who identify aggressiveness with efficacy. But it was the action of a frightened creature, lashing out at a perceived threat.

The shepherds, on the other hand, also faced fear. As they watched their flocks by night, and were all of the sudden surrounded by multitudes of the heavenly host, the old King James Version puts it, inimitably: "And the glory of the Lord shown round about them: and they were sore afraid" (Luke 2:9 KJV). If they had not been afraid, confident perhaps in their rods and staff to fight off these angels should they prove to be hostile, the shepherds would not have been courageous but, at best, self-deceived, and, at worst, insane. After feeling the fear, they heard the word from God meant to dispel it: "Fear not, for behold, I bring you good news of great joy that will be for all the people" (Luke 2:10). And that all leads to response: "When the angels went away from them into heaven, the shepherds said to one another, 'Let us go over to Bethlehem and see this thing that has happened, which the Lord has made known to us'" (Luke 2:15).

The pattern is fear leading to a word of consolation leading to a revelation. And while the revelations differ, in some ways, they all lead to the same conclusion—to the glory of Christ, often in unexpected places.

This is a pattern in the Scriptures. Isaiah, like the shepherds, saw the glory of God, and cried out in fear "Woe is me!" before God dispelled that fear with a word of mission (Isa. 6:5). Like the shepherds long after him, Isaiah's fear was brought on by a vision of glory. And that glory is not an abstract thing, but a person with a name, a face, and a blood type. John quoted from that account and wrote, "Isaiah said these things because he saw his glory and spoke of him" (John 12:41). But the story did not end there. "Nevertheless, many even of the authorities believed in him, but for fear of the Pharisees they did not confess it, so that they would not be put out of the synagogue" (John 12:42). What made the difference was not the presence of fear, but the sort of glory that motivated them: "for they loved the glory that comes from man more than the glory that comes from God" (John 12:43).

At the end of the day, that's where glory leaves us: either scared and running toward the glory of God, or scared and hiding underneath the glory of ourselves or of other people's opinions of us. The shepherds of Bethlehem were terrified, and we can only imagine why. "Fear not" does not need to be said by adorable winged babies, but by what the angels are, in fact, described to be, armies of fearsome warriors. When they told the tales of that night in the years to come, it must have sounded like, well, a scary ghost story, one that started in terror and ended in the shock-and-awe of an expanse filled with glory. That's completely consistent with the way God approaches all the rest of us. John told us, "The light shines in the darkness, and the darkness has not overcome it" (John 1:5). Even in his coming into this world, Jesus did not sidestep the darkness, the terror, of a world that is occupied by sin and death and the demonic. He walked right into that terror, and, with his own life and his own blood, upended it all. The only courage that can stand has to be built on that reality, not on any sort of natural fearlessness.

If courage were a lack of fear, then Jesus simply would have commended Simon Peter when he stepped out onto the storm-tossed waters of Galilee, walking out toward the Christ. But Jesus allowed him to sink momentarily beneath the waters, with the submerged fisherman screaming out in terror. Jesus said, "Do not be afraid" not because he was suggesting that Peter is incapable of drowning but instead because "It is I." Peter had to walk through fear to the other side of it, where Jesus stood. That was the case with Elijah too, and it will be the case with you. Elijah no doubt considered himself to be courageous, especially compared to those around him, and with good reason. Who else had challenged Ahab? Who else had put to flight an entire battalion of Baal worshippers? But in order to find the sustainable courage he would need, Elijah had to be brought beyond the limits of his self-sufficiency. He had to feel the fear, in order to find the courage where it really was—in a God who loves and stands by his children. The distinction is not between fearing and fearless people. The distinction is in what is feared: Jesus said, "Do not fear those who kill the body but cannot kill the soul. Rather fear him who can destroy both soul and body in hell" (Matt. 10:28). And the difference is where the fear leads—toward self-protection or toward faith. Only the latter is rightly called courage.

Viewing the Elijah story through social Darwinian eyes (the majority report in this age) one would no doubt conclude that Elijah was a coward while Ahab and Jezebel were courageous. He was the one feeling fear, and running away, while they were the ones taking decisive action. They were ordering military maneuvers while he was begging for death. But Ahab and Jezebel were cowards. The very reason the Baals existed in Israel was due to fear. Ahab and Jezebel were from two opposing nations, not because they were Romeo and Juliet star-crossed lovers, but as an act of pragmatic statecraft. The marriage was no doubt part of a geopolitical alliance meant to stave off hostilities, from one another and from other potentially hostile powers. Moreover, the people participating no doubt did so because they feared the royal house. They did not want what would happen to Elijah to happen to them—exile and presumed death. And, of course, there were (there always are) the court prophets, those who would tell the king precisely what he wanted to hear, for fear of losing their access, their influence, or their heads. That's cowardice.

Elijah was afraid. He was brought to the brink of that fear in the wilderness, and that's how Elijah found courage. He no doubt thought his time in the wilderness was an end point. On his better days, he probably assumed it was a cul-de-sac, a break from his main mission. But the wilderness is where Elijah was fitted for a quiet cross, which is the only place of safety to be found. That's what the wilderness was about for Elijah, and for you.

On his journey into the unknown, the Hobbit Frodo wondered how he could find the courage to keep walking, courage that others seemed to assume he had, but that he feared he didn't. "But where shall I find courage?" he asked. "That is what I chiefly need." The elf Gildor said to him, "Courage is found in unlikely places."[8] Indeed it is. Your courage will not come as you stand triumphantly on Mount Carmel, but when you find yourself collapsing in the wilderness, hearing the words, "What are you doing here, Elijah?" Elijah's path is yours too. He thought he was walking toward Mount Sinai, but he was really walking toward Mount Calvary. And so are you. Only the crucifiable self can find the courage to stand. That's where you are headed, no matter how scared and lost you feel. The way to courage is not without fear but through the fear, toward Christ.

As I look back on my boyhood trek through the haunted church, I am more convinced than ever that my uncle was right, though maybe not specifically in the way he meant it. There were demons in that church, and they were, in fact, chasing me. That's because the entire fallen cosmos "lies in the power of the evil one" (1 John 5:19). Places of holiness are often filled with the most dangers, and the places of the most danger are often where we find most clearly the holy presence of God. The theme of this universe is exactly what Flannery O'Connor identified as the theme of her fiction, namely, "the action of grace in territory held largely by the devil."[9] But we have been prepared for all this ahead of time.

Elijah was never reassured that Ahab and Jezebel were illusory threats, that they couldn't hurt him. They could. Elijah was never told that he was guaranteed safe passage through the wilderness, that he was strong enough for the task; just the opposite was the case. "Arise and eat," the angel said to the prophet, "for the journey is too great for you" (1 Kings 19:7). And the threat for us is even greater than a royal house of flesh-and-blood mortals. Jesus told Peter, "Simon, Simon, behold Satan demanded to have you, that he might sift you like wheat" (Luke 22:31). Simon Peter had to see, after his own sword-swinging and fireside-swearing and midnight running, that the answer for him was not that he had nothing to fear, but that the fears were answered by the one who stood on his behalf before the Father "that your faith may not fail" (Luke 22:32). Only after all of that, on the other side of the Devil's danger, on the other side of his own terror, could Peter "strengthen your brothers" (Luke 22:32).

Elijah was courageous because he learned how to be afraid in the right way. And so must you. You, like he, will walk through the valley of the shadow of death, and the only way you can learn to fear no evil is to conclude that someone is walking with you, someone is, in fact, shepherding you (Ps. 23), even when you cannot see him. We walk not around that valley but straight through it. That's how we learn that we can trust him. That's how we learn to be brave. The demons are there in the dark, that's true, but they are not the only things chasing you.

Goodness and mercy are too.

Chapter Three

# Courage and Shame

## *Freedom through Judgment*

"Life is short; have an affair." This advertising slogan became infamous not because of the success of its business but because of its collapse. The advertisement was on behalf of a dating service, which offered subscriptions for people to arrange extramarital sexual liaisons. The primary product offered by this company was not the technology to make an affair happen so much as it was the guarantee that one could keep it secret. The logo even featured a woman making a "hush" sign over her lips. Those lips didn't stay hushed, though, when a data breach leaked out the names and records of the service's subscribers, to the surprise (and horror) of a number of wives and husbands and employers and neighbors and friends. More than one minister was revealed to have used the service. At least one person was so distraught after being caught in this scandal that he was found dead by suicide. What was supposed to be cloaked in secrecy ended up exposed in shame.

Despite all the hype around this situation at the time, an adultery matching system, no matter how well advertised, will by nature only include a tiny number of people relative to the whole population. But it's useful to think about how the business model worked. The service was for people who wanted adultery without having to look like adulterers. The allure was that one could find a level of anonymity that was even more assured than trying to flirt with someone in a bar, where, theoretically, one could be overheard. By arranging all of this through a professional third party, one could be sure that, should one want it this way, the cheating partner might never even have to know the other person's name. And one could then continue on with regular life without anyone ever having to know that the marriage vows were broken, while also making sure one didn't have to die without experiencing the rush of cheating on a spouse. Life is short, after all.

This business did not have a keen sense of morality and ethics, but it did know human nature. In some sense, the drive behind this service is true of all of us, even those who would never think of breaking their promises to their spouses or families. Entertainment services have found, for instance, that they cannot rely on people to tell them what sorts of films and programs they like, because they will say they want highbrow art-films, which is the sort of movie they aspire to watch, rather than the raunchy comedies and romance flicks they actually watch. A consumer-made list often simply tells the kind of person the viewer wants to be; the algorithm reveals who he actually is.

Likewise, when people search online they are much less likely to preen or pretend, but instead to ask the questions they actually have. Since there is no audience, one feels freer to ask "What kind of headache means brain cancer?" without appearing to be a hypochondriac, or "How do I get rid of black mold in my bathroom?" without being thought of as unclean, or "Is it normal for my teenager to have a meth lab in his room?" without being judged as a bad parent.

When posting publicly, one study showed, women are likely to speak of their husbands as "awesome," while when they anonymously search for answers their questions are more often about why he has lost interest in sex or is so mean to them. That's why, this study revealed, mined data is more reliable than surveys and polls.[1] People don't always tell the truth to interviewers, or even to themselves, but when they think they are unseen and untracked, that's when the truth comes out. When the breach between who we pretend to be and who we really are becomes exposed, the result is shame.

For most of us, that shame is not being on a list of cheaters discovered in a technological glitch, but, in some way or the other, all of us know something of what it is to wonder if we are, in fact, who others think we are, who we pretend to be. Almost everyone has had the dream of walking through one's high school, and looking down, in shock and horror, to see that one is naked, having forgotten to dress that morning. Another common dream many people have is that there is a final examination coming up, and one forgot to study, or maybe even forgot to attend the classes altogether. My wife often dreams that she inadvertently has committed a crime, and is now being hauled off to the penitentiary by the police. The theme in dreams like these is exposure, of being found out by others.

That sense is not limited to the subconscious of the dream state, but, for many people, nags at them often in their lives. A term—"imposter syndrome"—was coined to describe this sense that one is really a fraud, that everything one has accomplished was a result of chance and luck, and that if people could really see into one's mind they would know that the person is not qualified to be doing what he or she is doing. That is not limited to one's sense of vocational qualification either. Most parents internally compare themselves to their own parents— who seemed so confident and sure of what to do—while they are, by contrast, second-guessing every decision they make in guiding their children. One woman told me that after she gave birth and was being wheeled out of the hospital with her baby she wondered if she had grounds to sue the hospital since they were sending a live infant off with someone as incompetent as she thought herself to be.

And that manifests itself in the spiritual arena too. Most Christians, at some point or other, fear that they are hypocrites, just like the religious leaders Jesus condemned. After all, if people could see into our hearts, and see the sorts of thoughts we have, the kind of distractions that come over us when we try to pray, they would see that we hardly measure up to the image we project. We know that other people have doubts, but we imagine they are not as paralyzing as ours. We know that everyone sins, but we assume that other people's sins are not quite as grotesque as our own. That is shame, and the path toward courage goes right through it.

The presenting issue for Elijah's flight into the wilderness was fear, a sense of external threat, and that much we can all immediately understand. We have locks on our doors for a reason. We install fire alarms for a purpose. But, once he is out there alone in the wilderness, the prophet's lament is not simply about his external circumstances—the bounty out on his head. Instead, all of that leads Elijah to a consideration not just of his situation but of himself. Sitting under a broom tree, he prayed for death, saying, "It is enough; now, O LORD, take away my life, for I am no better than my fathers" (1 Kings 19:4). Elijah here pronounced his own life to be a failure and, in a very real sense, conceded a key point to Ahab. The king, after all, had responded to the prophet not just with threats but also with shaming him. According to the king, he was a "troubler of Israel," disrupting the unity of the people of God (1 Kings 18:17). Elijah responded with the words, "I have not troubled Israel, but you have, and your father's house, because you have abandoned the commandments of the LORD and followed the Baals" (1 Kings 18:18).

The question at hand was a foretaste of Judgment Day, who is in the right, and who is in the wrong. Moreover, Elijah was announcing God's just judgment on the house of Ahab, seen in his withholding of rain from the land by his word, but by the time we get to the wilderness crisis, it is a live option that this judgment might kill Elijah before it affects Ahab. The servant of the Lord, not the peddlers of Baal, is the one who lies hungering and thirsting on the desert floor. Elijah is accused, and is hurtling toward, it appears, the wages of sin: death.

For Elijah, the problem was not just what was outside of him, but the problem was him. Elijah despaired that he was to die "for I am no better than my fathers" (1 Kings 19:4). He lamented that he was the only one faithful who was left, and that he would soon be killed (1 Kings 19:14). He couldn't outrun the royal family forever. He was just a man. He looked at his own life and mission, and pronounced it all a failure. He stood self-accused. In that sense, he was declaring that Ahab had been right all along, not about Baal, but about Elijah. They both had concluded that the prophet needed to die in shame.

In order to see what this moment means for you, you must first diagnose what exactly Elijah was up against. It was not, to use the traditional Christian formulation, simply "the world" and "the flesh," although as we saw earlier, it was certainly that. Elijah here, though, was also grappling with the Devil. Now, you might stop at this point and note that the Devil nowhere appears in this text, and of course that's true. In fact, this being is nowhere mentioned in the Elijah storyline, which might lead us to conclude that Satan is absent. But, as always, the Devil is in the details.

Elijah, after all, stood accused. And in order to see the work of the Devil in Elijah's story, and in ours, we must see where the Devil's primary power lay, and it's not in jumping out from behind bushes to alarm human beings. The Devil is not a warrior as much as a guerilla terrorist, and his strategy is that of intimidation through accusation. He is the mysterious spiritual Adversary of Scripture who accuses us "day and night before our God" (Rev. 12:10). The most effective means of this accusation is not when the accusations are false, but when they are true.

I do many question-and-answer sessions on university and college campuses, and often take questions from atheists who disagree completely with my beliefs. Most of them are civil, kind, and interesting people, asking good-faith (no pun intended) questions meant to clarify not to confront. But, once in a while, an atheist will be hostile, and accuse me, as one did, of having "an imaginary friend named Jesus." This does not bother me at all, mostly because I know that if I were to conjure up an imaginary friend he would be far less irritating in his demands of me than Jesus has turned out to be. My blood pressure doesn't elevate, and I hardly think about the "accusation" when I'm thinking through the day as I try to find sleep that night.

But I was tortured by a question, a bit ago, that was not meant to be hostile at all. The questioner, a Christian, asked, "You travel a lot, and you have five children; how do you balance all of that?" Again, the question was a good one, and the questioner was just trying to get a sense of how to balance his own schedule with competing demands. But it stung. I felt defensive inside and tried not to display it. That season I had travelled too much, had missed too many ballgames and school plays. He wasn't accusing me of anything, but I felt accused by myself, and it hurt not because that accusation was false but because it was true. Now, the Devil knows this. Yes, the Devil is, as Jesus told us, one who "is a liar and the father of lies" (John 8:44). When it comes to the Devil's first power over us—deception—this sort of craftiness is a useful tool. But when it comes to his final power over us—that of accusation—his strength is not in his cunning but in his honesty. The Devil tells us lies about the consequences of sin, until we are guilty, and then he prosecutes us unrelentingly for that sin.

For most of human history, human beings have had some concept of a devil, or of dark spirits at work in the cosmos, but in our time few do. The very idea is seen as an outmoded aspect of premodern superstition. And yet, the Devil's power of accusation does not lose its grip just because people do not think he exists. To see this, simply notice what happens on an airplane when an unexpected wave of turbulence sends the craft spinning through the air. Even a committed naturalist, who might tell you that death is simply non-existence, a permanent dreamless sleep, and that human life is just a matter of atoms banging together, probably will scream. He is not fearing the pain of death; he knows he will lose consciousness before the plane hits the ground if it is to crash. Perhaps what is at work in that terror is simply animal instinct, the life-protection impulse at work in every living being with a higher-level nervous system. Perhaps. But perhaps the fear of death is about something much more. That's the Bible's claim: for human beings, fear of death isn't just about physical expiration but about something else besides—an unarticulated "fearful expectation of judgment" (Heb. 10:27).

Why would there be a fear of judgment even in people who don't believe that there's a God, or an afterlife, or even an objective standard for right and wrong? That's because, at least at the core of the psyche, no such person exists. The apostle Paul taught that every human person is embedded with a knowledge of God, a knowledge activated by the creation itself (Rom. 1:18–21). The claim is not just that people ought to be able to know there is a God, if they traced back the evidence from the design of nature, or what have you. No, the claim is stronger than that. This knowledge is not cognitive information-bearing, the knowing that there is a God, but personal knowledge—"For although they knew God, they did not honor him as God or give thanks to him" (Rom. 1:21). This refusal of worship leads then to a suppression of the truth, to a kind of self-hypnosis.

Moreover, the claim is that every human conscience is embedded with the knowledge of good and evil, the criteria by which we will be judged on the last day (Rom. 2:14–16). We all, apart from the gospel, seek to suppress this knowledge, both of how we are sinning and also that there might be a day of accounting for it all. The result is a sort of generalized anxiety. Apart from Christ, we are in slavery, the Bible says, to fear (Rom. 8:15). "Since therefore the children share in flesh and blood, he himself likewise partook of the same things," the Bible says of Jesus, "that through death he might destroy the one who has the power of death, that is, the devil, and deliver all those who through fear of death were subject to lifelong slavery" (Heb. 2:14–15). Most people, as Blaise Pascal put it, find "distractions" to keep them occupied from such questions—distractions of work or play or love or resentment or even religion and the pursuit of truth and justice. We do so because we are scared.[2] And yet, as anyone can say who has been in "denial" about a cheating spouse or a predatory work environment, even the heartiest self-deception will come bubbling to the surface at unpredictable, inconvenient times, and if it is to be held down must be supplemented with even more self-deception.

In the wilderness, Elijah's defenses were routed. He judged his life's project a failure, and sought to get it all over with quickly. He wanted to die. What he encountered, though, was not an end-run around judgment, but a confrontation with it, face-to-face. God approached this man and said to him, "What are you doing here, Elijah?" (1 Kings 19:9, 13).

And the same is, and will be, true for you. A key barrier to courage is shame, a sense of judgment. The apostle John wrote this: "By this is love perfected with us, so that we may have confidence for the day of judgment, because as he is so also are we in this world. There is no fear in love, but perfect love casts out fear. For fear has to do with punishment, and whoever fears has not been perfected in love. We love because he first loved us" (1 John 4:17–19). This is key. The way out of shame is not around judgment, but right through it.

In fact, for Elijah, the confrontation with God at this point of shame actually returned him to his starting point, the place where we found the prophet in the story in the first place. When he announced the judgment of God on the house of Ahab, Elijah said to the king, "As the LORD, the God of Israel, lives, before whom I stand, there shall be neither dew nor rain these years, except by my word" (1 Kings 17:1). The words are crucial—"before whom I stand." Elijah did not come with any personal authority or personal credibility. He was not even, at that point, established as any sort of miracle-worker. He was just an obscure peasant from a backwater place. But he had standing before the Lord.

Now that language of "standing" is often confused for us, especially when said in the context of courage. We think of "standing" as self-confidence and assertiveness. "I won't stand for that," we might say, or "You may knock me down, but I will always stand back up," or "Here's where I stand." Often, in our era, to "stand" for something means to offer a loud expression of opinion. To be sure, there are some uses of this language in Scripture that are consistent with this sort of meaning. One of King David's mighty men, for instance, "took his stand" against a plot by the Philistine enemies, killing them (1 Chron. 11:14). Elijah's meaning here, though, is not about his personal authority but about his personal accountability. This has to do with where his ultimate judgment lay, and that was before the face of the living God.

The idea of "standing" has to do with submitting oneself to scrutiny, and surviving that scrutiny. The wicked, the psalmist wrote, "will not stand in the judgment" (Ps. 1:5). Elsewhere David sang, "Who shall ascend the hill of the LORD? And who shall stand in his holy place?" (Ps. 24:3), and again "If you, O LORD, should mark iniquities, O Lord, who could stand?" (Ps. 130:3). The prophet Malachi, just as he was to prophesy of the return of Elijah, noted that the Lord would return to his temple, and that this is not necessarily good news for everybody. "But who can endure the day of his coming, and who can stand when he appears?" (Mal. 3:2). The New Testament uses the same sort of language. Jesus stood in judgment before Pilate. Paul stood in judgment before Caesar, but both of them spoke of a more ultimate standing before God. "Who are you to pass judgment on the servant of another?" Paul wrote to the church at Rome. "It is before his own master that he stands or falls. And he will be upheld, for the Lord is able to make him stand" (Rom. 14:4). That's precisely the point.

Elijah knew that, as a prophet, he was accountable before God for his words, what he said and what he refused to say (Deut. 18:15 22). God is the One "before whom I stand," Elijah was saying to the king, "and therefore you are not." This is the truth, the Scripture will reveal, not just for as exceptional a figure as Elijah, but every one of us. That's why Paul can say that he could have "good courage" in light of that certainty: "For we must all appear before the judgment seat of Christ, so that each one may receive what is due for what he has done in the body, whether good or evil," Paul wrote (2 Cor. 5:10).

I recognize that it seems insane to suggest that the antidote to a culture of shame is the Judgment Seat of Christ, that judgment can drive us toward courage. Judgment is, after all, terrifying and shame-inducing. I've written elsewhere about the horror with which I read, as a small child, an illustrated fundamentalist Christian tract, picturing a dead man on Judgment Day, standing before God on a throne. A film was shown, in front of everyone there, detailing back every sin he had ever committed, whether large or small. "This was your life," said an angel next to the throne. I blushed with shame, even though I look back and think of how few, and how boring, my sins at the time would have been. But the thought of having my parents, my school friends, and Jesus, watch that life, seemed to me worse than hell. Most people would laugh at that tract, but virtually everyone grapples at some point with the feelings it evokes.

That should not surprise biblical theists. When primal humanity fell into sin, the initial thing they could sense was their own shame—naked before each other, hiding from the voice of God (Gen. 3:8–10). We hide our brokenness from each other, and even from ourselves. That's why Jeremiah said,

"The heart is deceitful above all things, and desperately sick; who can understand it?" (Jer. 17:9). Even when people appear to be happy and confident and self-assured, they are churning with resentment, fear, and shame, even if they can't articulate why that is. But to cope, people tend to reassure themselves that they can cover their tracks before God, and before others. Not everyone says, "There is no God." But, even when not, we tell ourselves, "The LORD does not see; the God of Jacob does not perceive" (Ps. 94:7). That's why, I think, that tract was so scary to me, because it detailed graphically something that I intuitively knew was true about God and about myself, namely that "no creature is hidden from his sight, but all are naked and exposed to the eyes of him to whom we must give account" (Heb. 4:13). Both Ahab and Elijah would ultimately stand before the tribunal of God. But only Elijah knew it. And that's what made the difference for him.

The way this works is actually not the way implied in the tract I read, or in the way most people think about judgment, which is to say that looking forward to the Judgment Seat is meant to dissuade us from misbehavior by teaching us to fear punishment, the way that the death penalty is thought by some to be a deterrent against capital crimes. Yes, the Scriptures warn people of the day when God will judge the world (Acts 17:31). This was a key part of the preaching of prophets such as Elijah and those in his line, including John the Baptist. When the apostle Paul gained an audience with the governor Felix, Paul reasoned with him about "righteousness and self-control and the coming judgment" to the point that the governor was alarmed and changed the subject (Acts 24:25). None of this though is presented as if it were information that was new to any human being. We all, like old Felix, are trying to change the subject.

God has shown himself to all of us, in a creation that is embedded with signs pointing to him (Rom. 1:18–21). More than that, God has embedded within the human conscience an awareness of his law in a way that points people to the day when "God judges the secrets of men by Christ Jesus" (Rom. 2:16). Left to ourselves, though, we suppress all of that, and follow the path of our own inclinations, convincing ourselves that we will never be found out, until all that remains in our consciousness is a kind of inchoate angst. The gospel changes all of that, though.

When we are united to Christ, we are no longer to cringe before the thought of Judgment Day. That's because we no longer have the pressure to make the case for our own innocence. Our case is thoroughly debunked. At the cross, God has already revealed our guilt. In our repentance from sin, we have already agreed with his verdict, and our ongoing confession of sin reaffirms that agreement. Judgment Day happened for us, in a very real sense, already, at the Place of the Skull outside the gates of Jerusalem two millennia ago.

At the cross, Jesus was crucified not just in torture but also in shame. His clothes ripped apart for the gambling glee of some soldiers, Jesus was naked before the crowds. Not only that, he was humiliated as powerless before the Roman Empire and, more importantly, seen as a lawbreaker under the curse of God (Deut. 21:22–23; Gal. 3:10–14). That's why Paul reiterated so often that he was "not ashamed of the gospel" (Rom. 1:16). He was not attempting to communicate that he wasn't bashful to tell people that he followed Christ, although that's certainly true. He was saying that he was not shrinking back in shame about what everyone at the time would have seen as shameful: the execution of a "troubler of Israel" (and of Israel-occupying Rome) on a Roman instrument of torture.

Jesus, "who for the joy that was set before him endured the cross, despising the shame" is the one who is now "seated at the right hand of the throne of God" (Heb. 12:2). If we are united to Christ, we have been to both places. We were with him, "outside the gate" at the cross: "Therefore, let us go to him outside the camp and bear the reproach he endured" (Heb. 13:13). And, in Christ, we have been raised from the dead and exalted to the right hand of God. Judgment Day, then, is not some foreboding assessment of whether God is for us or against us. As the Spirit has said to us, "Who shall bring any charge against God's elect? It is God who justifies. Who is to condemn? Christ Jesus is the one who died—more than that, who was raised—who is at the right hand of God" (Rom. 8:33–34). The good news is that the cross has already revealed to us our Judgment Day, both in the condemnation of our sin there and also in God's verdict of righteousness as we are hidden in Christ Jesus. That frees us from shame.

What strikes me as a I reread the Gospel of John is the theme there of Jesus' knowing awareness of all who were around him. Jesus, John said, "knew all people and needed no one to bear witness about man, for he himself knew what was in man" (John 2:24–25). What is perhaps most startling to me about Jesus' reaction to sinners in the Gospels is not just that he forgives them, but how he is not shocked by whatever it is they are hiding, for good or for ill. Jesus pronounces Nathanael "an Israelite indeed, in whom there is no deceit" (John 1:47). That's a positive act of judgment, to be sure, but not one that Nathanael was initially willing to appreciate. After all, who takes seriously a commendation from someone who knows nothing about the person being commended? That changes when Jesus reveals that he knew Nathanael when "under the fig tree, I saw you" (John 1:48). Jesus similarly reveals how much he knows about a seeming stranger when he tells the Samaritan woman at the well that he knows about her sin: "you have had five husbands, and the one you now have is not your husband" (John 4:18). The astounding part of this is that Jesus knew this already when he invited her to drink of the living water of life he offers. They both asked a version the same question, "How do you know me?" (John 1:48). We would do well to ask the same.

God is not waiting for an after-death data-dump to tell him who we are. He knows. He was not surprised by the backstory of the prostitutes and tax collectors with whom he ate. He told Simon Peter about his betrayal before Peter could even believe that he was capable of such a thing.

And the same is true for you.

The point is not that Jesus can see past your "imposter syndrome" to know who you really are behind all of it, although that's true. The point is that, knowing all of that, God sent his Son to die for you (Rom. 5:8).

Jesus knew all about the people he sought out—bumbling frauds and scandalous criminals alike—and he sought them out anyway.

The same is true for you.

Wherever you heard the gospel—whether on a parent's lap reading a nighttime Bible story or in a booklet left on a subway train or in a conversation with an acquaintance in a coffee shop—all of that happened in the plotline of a sovereign God who as Lord of history is mysteriously bending the plotline of the cosmos toward himself. Wherever you heard the gospel, you were not overhearing some abstract claim. You were hearing something you were intended to hear, from someone or something that was—probably without even knowing it—sent to you. And Jesus knew all about whatever you're ashamed of, whatever you're trying to hide, whatever it is about yourself that makes you feel too scared to stand.

Judgment Day frees us from shame because, through the gospel, we no longer try to hide from God, as our prehistoric ancestors did before us. That voice, "Adam, where are you?" that once drove a sinful humanity to hide in shame in the bushes still goes forth. But we now stand in Jesus, who answers that voice confidently, "Behold, I and the children God has given me" (Heb. 2:13). We are hidden in him now—and we will be hidden in him on the day we stand before that Judgment Seat, and every day between now and then. We are free then to confess our sin, boldly, knowing that Jesus forgives us, intercedes for us, and is not one bit shocked by us.

That reality doesn't lead to presumption but to accountability. We don't hide our sins and vulnerabilities and temptations. With a long enough view into the future, we know we ultimately can't. We don't cover ourselves to save face. We don't seek refuge in the shadows. Darkness is where, in fact, these evils latch onto us. We shine light on our own darkness, confess our sins to one another and to God, seek help for others to bear our burdens with us. Knowing this about ourselves helps to rid us of judgmental attitudes about the sins and struggles of others. Paul asked the church at Rome, "Why do you pass judgment on your brother? Or you, why do you despise your brother? For we will all stand before the judgment seat of God; for it is written, 'As I live, says the Lord, every knee shall bow to me, and every tongue shall confess to God.' So then each of us will give an account of himself to God. Therefore let us not pass judgment on one another any longer, but rather decide never to put a stumbling block or hindrance in the way of a brother" (Rom. 14:10–13). Knowing we will be judged along with everyone else gives us compassion. Knowing that God will judge frees us from having to do so ourselves.

We are hidden in him. He knows all about us, and came looking for us anyway. We have nothing left to fear, nothing left to hide. If we have nothing to fear but God himself, and if God has already pronounced that anyone in Christ is freed from all condemnation, then what do we have to fear? Nothing. That's what the psalmist meant when he wrote, "The LORD is my light and my salvation; whom shall I fear? The LORD is the strong-hold of my life; of whom shall I be afraid?" (Ps. 27:1). And that is another way of saying what the apostle Paul asked, "If God is for us, who can be against us?" (Rom. 8:31). That's why the Scripture grounds courage in the "expectation and hope that I will not be at all ashamed" (Phil. 1:20).

But the shame we bear, the shame that is a stumbling block to live a life of courage, is not just shame before God, but also shame before other people. Now, on first glance, the notion of "judgment" is noxious to most people around us. If you asked a typical group of unbelievers what they hate about religious people, one of the first answers to come up would be that the religious are "judgmental." Sometimes even people who might not know a single other Bible verse will be able to cite Jesus' words "Judge not lest ye be judged," even usually quoting them just like that, in the old King James lingo. And these skeptics of religion certainly have a point. No doubt they have all experienced Christians acting morally superior to the people around them, and holding others to standards to which they do not hold themselves. But our era has not actually moved beyond "judgment" at all.

Even the denunciation of judgmental attitudes is based on a kind of "judgment," if we define judgment as a discernment between what is good and what is evil. Authenticity is judged to be good, and hypocrisy to be evil. And, so far as it goes, all that is true. No person could act coherently without some sense of justice, some distinction between what is moral and immoral, even if we disagree sharply on what those distinctions are. Ironically, though, a sense of the Judgment Seat of Christ is exactly what our culture needs the most, and it does not, in fact, lead to judgmental attitudes but away from them. "For what have I to do with judging outsiders?" the apostle Paul wrote. "Is it not those inside the church whom you are to judge?" (1 Cor. 5:12). Why is this the case? "God judges those outside" (1 Cor. 5:13). The church is freed from acting as rulers over the outside world, ripping the weeds up from among the crops or separating out the goats away from the sheep, precisely because we know there is a future Day of Judgment to come, and that we will not be the ones on the throne there.

And it simply is not true that we live in a time without judgment, no matter how we may want to view ourselves. Our age has not replaced the Judgment Seat of Christ with nothing but with a countless number of little judgment seats. Not only this, but the ultimate penalty of those judgment seats is the dispensing of shame and exile. Whether in a middle school cafeteria or in a theological seminary faculty lounge or in a nursing home game room, the ultimate punishment is to be told, "You are not one of us; go away." That is shame. And the fear of that kind of shame leads people to hide themselves in whatever crowd they need in order to belong.

This is just as likely to happen within the church as anywhere else, maybe more so. We are commanded to be separate from sin, never separate from sinners. It is far easier to do the reverse. And the charge, "He eats with tax collectors and sinners" still works. Courage means not fearing those who will seek to intimidate you from following Christ toward those who are sick and in need of a physician. Clearly, the Scriptures call us to judge those on the inside, who bear the name of brother, and not those on the outside. Doing the reverse can make for a much easier ministry, as a hack.

The Judgment Seat, when rightly understood, obliterates all of that. Freedom from shame before God can lead to freedom from shame before others. Consider what the apostle Paul wrote to his critics in Corinth: "But with me it is a very small thing that I should be judged by you or by any human court" (1 Cor. 4:3). At first glance, this sort of mentality seems attractive to our ambient culture, because it sounds like a sort of "You can't judge me!" defiance, in favor of an autonomous quest for personal authenticity. Nothing could be further from this, though. Paul continued: "In fact, I do not even judge myself. For I am not aware of anything against myself, but I am not thereby acquitted. It is the Lord who judges me. Therefore, do not pronounce judgment before the time, before the Lord comes, who will bring to light the things now hidden in darkness and will disclose the purposes of the heart" (1 Cor. 4:3–5). Paul did not find freedom from other people's opinions of him because he was unaccountable to judgment but because he was. He understood that his own knowledge of himself was ultimately a mystery to himself, much less to others.

Sometimes we can trace back something about why we do the things that we do, but most of the time we can't trace all of that out, and if we try to sort through all of our own motives and hidden intentions we end up in a labyrinth with no exit. But we do not need to know everything that is going on inside of us in order to pursue holiness and obedience. Indeed, much of what is pictured at the Judgment Seat in the Gospels is a mystery to those involved. Sometimes the passage in Matthew 25—of Jesus as shepherd separating the sheep from the goats, those who gain eternal life from those who are to experience condemnation— can be unsettling to Christians. After all, Jesus said that the criteria for the distinction between these two is that the "sheep" recognized him in the hungry, the naked, the imprisoned, the stranger as they cared for them, while the "goats" did not. The point of Jesus' teaching, though, is that what matters in light of the kingdom is not what seems to matter in this fallen universe, red in tooth and claw, obsessed with status and prestige.

In Jesus' teaching on the Judgment Seat, the "sheep" are seen to be so not because of their visible impressiveness (even impressiveness in the way they serve the needy); the goats have that. Rather, they are seen to be "sheep" because they knew Christ, and followed him where he led. Jesus said, "Truly, I say to you, as you did it to one of the least of these my brothers, you did it to me" (Matt. 25:40). But this comes as a surprise not only to the damned but to the redeemed. The "sheep" do not recognize themselves in Jesus' pronouncements about them: "Lord, when did we see you hungry and feed you or thirsty and give you drink?" We do not even have a good read on our own lives, much less on anyone else's.

But thinking carefully about our own lives is important. *New York Times* columnist David Brooks famously distinguished between "résumé virtues" (our accomplishments in career or with money or fame) and our "eulogy virtues" (those aspects of our character that people will remember when we die, which he, rightly, argues are more important).[3] But the "eulogy virtues" can be hard to discern from the inside out. We all know someone of whom we would say, "That person just lacks self-knowledge." To some degree or other, all of us do. But beyond this, though, at the end of our lives, more important than our "résumé virtues" and our "eulogy virtues" would be a Judgment Seat proclamation: "Well done, good and faithful servant" (Matt. 25:23). When we find this in Christ, we can start to see what matters and what doesn't, and we can also start to see that much of what we thought mattered came about as we imitated the people around us or sought, consciously or unconsciously, their approval.

A parent of an adolescent told me recently that she was befuddled by her daughter's seemingly contradictory impulses toward being an individual and belonging. "She seems to want me to be close to her and yet to be free of me, all at the same time," the parent said. "It's hard to know whether I should come in closer, or step back and give her space, because I don't think she even knows which she wants." To some degree, this is not just an adolescent struggle but one we all face all life long. That's because, as writer Ziyad Marar observes, all of us are driven by two contradictory impulses: the need to be free and the need to be justified. He defines "freedom" as a sense of control and agency and self-determination, and he defines justification as "a desire for belonging and applause."[4] In previous cultures, Marar argues, this need for justification was found chiefly in gods or traditions, but in our secularizing age we can find it only in each other.[5] The way to happiness comes in finding some synthesis to these contradictory needs. But the shadow side of this kind of "freedom" is isolation and aloneness, and the shadow side of this kind of "justification" is that whatever group can applaud one can also reject one with shame.

This gatekeeping power of shame is what culture and technology writer Seth Godin targets when he argues that the fear of criticism leads to mediocrity at best and creative paralysis at worst. "Tribes seek to shame those who act or look different," he writes. "When those in power use shame to bully the weak into compliance, they are stealing from us. They tell us that they will expose our secrets (not good enough, not hardworking enough, not from the right family, made a huge mistake once) and will use the truth to exile us from our tribe. This shame, the shame that lives deep within us, is used as a threat."[6] People respond to this sort of fear of shame by just laying low, not stepping outside whatever boundaries might expose them to exile. Most of the time this is not due to an explicit threat, Jezebel's promise to murder Elijah, for instance, but is unspoken.

Someone once told me about their house growing up and learning to tiptoe through the family room because, often, the father was passed out drunk on the sofa there. No one ever mentioned the father's drinking, and no one directed the children to remain in silence in the middle of the day. It was the unspoken means of staying in the tribe. But all that leads to is stifling conformity, the shutting down of ideas and gifts that could bless the world. The answer, Godin argues, is to choose the right audience. Knowing your audience will tell you, he argues, whom to target and from whom to receive feedback and whom to ignore. "If you don't pinpoint your audience, you end up making your art for the loudest, crankiest critics," he writes. "And that's a waste."[7]

Conformity leads, ultimately, to cynicism because the pull of the crowd is not governed by truth but by fear. As philosopher Søren Kierkegaard noted, "The majority of people are not so afraid of holding a wrong opinion as they are of holding an opinion alone."[8]

That pull toward conformity is not limited to certain areas, but manifests in nearly every aspect of ordinary life—your job, your relationships, your parenting or being parented. No one will please everyone all the time. As a friend said to me once, "Never agonize over criticism from people you wouldn't go to for advice." But, even so, there's more to shame than project-by-project work. There's the larger, more existential question, of whether the efforts, in shaming your words or your work are rooted in an overall shamefulness not just of what you do or what you think, but who you are.

The answer to shame cannot be denial about shameful acts. You are, after all, a child of Adam, part of a fallen humanity driven in reality into shame. And you, personally, have done countless shameful things. You might be willing to find courage by overcoming shame in specific issues, but to find the courage to live out your life you must go to the root of shame. You must bear it, or rather, you must see who bore it for you. Only an already-judged person can do this. Only a crucified person can do this.

That's why the apostle Paul could carry out his mission despite being mischaracterized and slandered: "For am I now seeking the approval of man, or of God?" (Gal. 1:10). And that's why Jesus did not flinch when he stood before the "judgment seat" of Pilate (Matt. 27:19; John 19:13). Jesus knew that the real Judgment Seat was to come, and that the roles there would be reversed. We do not then need to find approval from the crowd around us, or the crowd in our heads. We do not need to compare our lives with others. Nor do we need to justify ourselves and answer every lie or slander or false accusation or criticism. Jesus told his disciples that they would be "dragged before governors and kings for my sake" (Matt. 10:18), that they would be maligned and put out of their communities. And yet he told them not to "be anxious how you are to speak, or what you are to say" (Matt. 10:19). Why? Jesus pointed his disciples to find their identity in him, not in their standing before any human tribunal, and he pointed them to the Judgment Seat. "So have no fear of them, for nothing is covered that will not be revealed, or hidden that will not be known" (Matt. 10:26).

Knowing the "fear of the Lord," then, we are freed from the fear of people, freed from shame. Anything short of that just leaves us ashamed and afraid, because that sort of approval from people, even when found, is fleeting and exhausting to maintain, and hardly the same thing as a Father who really knows you for who you are and loves you anyway. Freedom from shame comes through judgment.

That's how Elijah was able to stand boldly before Ahab; because he already saw himself as standing before God. The wilderness crisis led him back to a face-to-face meeting with shame, not to leave him there, but to take him back to that sense of identity and calling. The same will be true for you. Good news—Judgment Day is coming. Even better news— Judgment Day has already come. And here you stand, hidden in Christ, hearing the verdict pronounced over you that was pronounced long ago over the waters of Jordan and again at an empty garden tomb: "This is my beloved child, in whom I am well-pleased." The criterion is not the strength of your faith— weak and wavering as it no doubt is—but rather, the criterion is the Life to which that faith has joined you, the crucifiable but irrepressible life of Jesus.

Life is short; don't be ashamed.

Chapter Four

# Courage and Integrity

## *Wholeness through Brokenness*

Pretending to be a doctor is a crime, but no one would have prosecuted this old man. For one thing, he wasn't really pretending. He had been to medical school, had a medical license, and had decades and decades of medical experience. As a matter of fact, he was at the top of his field, at least at one time, the director of a prestigious hospital treating patients with dementia and other aging-related cognitive diseases. This man would have known exactly how to deal with patients who didn't remember him from one visit to the other, even if those visits were within hours of each other. The cruel irony, though, is that when Oliver Sacks introduces us to his colleague in one of his books, the man is now elderly, and afflicted with dementia himself, the very disease he had spent a lifetime combatting, and is placed in the very hospital he had once served as director. The man, though, didn't know this. The surroundings were familiar to him, and so was the routine, so every day he would make his rounds, checking in with patients, examining their charts, and making notes to himself about their progress. He was no longer supposed to practice medicine. But no one told him otherwise. The patients no doubt didn't know any better themselves, and the hospital personnel probably thought it was best for the man to live in his illusion.

All that came to an end, though, when one day while making rounds on the floor, the man flipped through the chart beside an empty bed. He read the diagnosis of advanced dementia, along with the list of symptoms and test results. Then he saw the patient's name at the top of the chart, and the name was his own. "That's me," the man cried out. "God help me!"[1]

What was at stake for this elderly man was a question of integrity. That word seems not to fit because we tend to think of integrity only in terms of moral judgments—"She is so two-faced; she lacks all integrity," etc. And that's certainly part of it. But here I mean integrity, first, in a much more literal sense, in what it means to hold together, to make sense as a coherent whole. In the life of this man, he faced a crisis related to truth— the truth about how he saw the world around him, and, as a result, the truth about who he was. The hospital notes revealed that the situation wasn't what it seemed, and he wasn't what he seemed.

That's our challenge too.

If you spied on our house on any given day, you might well hear something like the following conversation: "Samuel and Jonah are over at Moses's house, with Isaac, and then Jeremiah's mother will drive them to Daniel's house." Names come and go, to be sure, but in no era I can think of has the name "Jezebel" come into fashion for little girls. And I haven't encountered any men named "Ahab" either, though that may have more to do with Herman Melville's obsessed sea captain than with biblical literacy. But prophets are a different story. As I write this, the server in the coffee shop where I'm sitting is wearing a nametag marked "Zephaniah." The young man at the cash register wears one that reads "Micah." This probably wouldn't be the case if I lived in Portland or Santa Barbara, but I live in suburban Nashville, still isolated enough from secularizing trends to be a Bible Belt. Add to that the particular ecosystem in which we live, between the church where we worship and the homeschooling co-op my children attend, and there are biblical names all over the place.

Much of this has to do with the sheer number of options available to parents who go to the Bible for name ideas. There are a few options from the patriarchs and matriarchs (a "Jacob" or a "Rebekah," for instance) and from the New Testament followers of Jesus. But there are very few children named for biblical kings and queens. Sure, there will always be boys named "David" and occasionally girls named "Esther." The name "Solomon" comes and goes, with parents in Bible-reading homes no doubt bracing for the day when the little one asks, "Mom, what's a concubine?" The name "Josiah" is a good option, and maybe, if people weren't thinking about how long it would take to learn to spell one's name, "Hezekiah." But, beyond that, the options narrow drastically, given the depressing picture of the moral and spiritual lives of these rulers in the Old Testament.

That bleak picture is, if anything, heightened when we come to the Elijah story. Ahab, the Scripture tells us, "did evil in the sight of the LORD, more than all who were before him" (1 Kings 16:30). And that's saying something, given all who came before him. Still, when up against Ahab and Jezebel, Elijah had every reason to despair. The royal house had more than just an army and a treasury. They had the ability to shape what reality was in their domain. They could define right and wrong, truth and falsehood. All that the prophet had was a word from God. This was a question of integrity, and the courage to face the future stood or fell on that.

When it comes to your own struggle for courage, this probably seems quite different from your situation. After all, a death-penalty-threatening queen is not likely chasing you into the woods.

But the fundamental problem is still the same. In order to stand with courage, you must know what is, in fact, real and what is fake, what is true and what is false. And in every era and in every place, the tendency will be to define truth according to the will of the powerful or the whims of the crowd rather than according to something that transcends all of that. Whether in a family or in a workplace or even in a church, you will face the pressure to grow silent about certain things, or even to ignore reality itself, in order to save yourself the trouble of being out of step with someone who can hurt you, or with where the conventional wisdom is. The end result of that is a conscience that no longer knows how to tell the difference between good and evil, only between "safe" and "scary," between "useful" and "inconvenient."

The ways of God are different. That's why the skirmish between prophet and king is not usually fought in some sort of geopolitical arena, as in the case with Elijah, but much more often in the staging ground of the human psyche. You do not need to have a Jezebel seeking your blood in order to be tempted to trade away truth for safety. All you need is whoever or whatever it is that you fear in front of you. And then the question will be what sort of integrity has come together in you, to prepare you for that moment.

Most who name their children after prophets do so to honor their child's namesake (and because they *like* the name). Christians generally tend to see the prophets as being commendable but inimitable heroes, distant from our own circumstances. But if that is you, realize that you are probably closer to standing where they stood than you might have previously imagined. The language of "prophet" and "prophetic" is skewed in our time, as are lots of other biblical words. "Pastoral," for instance, has come to mean, at least for many people, a passive and conflict-averse personality. "He would never call out the predatory payday loan-shark in his church for their racketeering and human trafficking," one might say. "He's too pastoral." In reality, though, "pastoral" means the exact reverse, rooted in the language of the shepherd who fought off predators and who would carry out dangerous expeditions to rescue an imperiled animal.

"Discernment," similarly, has been co-opted by buffoonish conspiracy theorists and heresy-hunters broadcasting often-fabricated aspersions against any authority they can find, when the word, biblically defined, means the wisdom to know what is true and what is fake.

In like manner, the word *prophet* is often reserved for overconfident evangelists predicting falsely the end of the world around every corner. And, on a smaller scale, the word *prophetic* is reserved for people who are just naturally quarrelsome. Often the person drawn to the word *prophetic* always sees himself as Elijah versus Ahab or Augustine versus Pelagius or Martin Luther versus the Pope, when, in reality, this person would be just as passionately fighting if he were a Zen Buddhist in a meditation compound ("That guru is not really Enlightened!") or a vegan in an animal rights group ("Vegetarianism is not pure enough! Eating dairy is forced labor!"). For such people, religion is merely a prop to furnish the room. It serves as little more than background, a setting for the pugilist to exercise his angst under the guise of spiritual fervor. The zeal of this would-be prophet is not the Spirit, but the limbic system.

This problem was compounded by the popular use of "spiritual gifts inventories" in churches over the past few generations, when the New Testament gift of "prophet" was often assigned to people who enjoyed pointing out flaws and arguing about stuff. But that's not the picture we have of the prophets themselves. They are hardly self-assertive and self-confident, but rather are more often reluctant and even terrified. That's because "prophetic" does not refer to a personality type but to a carried word. And that's why the calling of the prophet has to do with your own integrity and courage, regardless of your disposition or what your spiritual gifts may be.

Looking at the Bible, Christians over the centuries have pointed out the distinct offices of prophet, priest, and king, offices that were essential to the ordering of the people of Israel and offices that all came to their climax in the person of Jesus of Nazareth. If you are in Christ, the Bible teaches that you share in his calling and in his inheritance, which means, in a very qualified and derivative sense, you share in something of all three of these offices. The office of king was set up to maintain order internally (think of Solomon judging the dispute between the two women over which one was the real mother of the surviving baby) and to provide for the defense of the people externally (think of David fighting off the Philistines). Jesus, from the house of David, is the rightful King of Israel and of the whole universe. And those who belong to him, Jesus says, will rule and reign with him in the age to come (Luke 22:28–30). The temptation, though, is always for Christians to assume that because they reign with Christ in heaven that they are now to be in charge of the outside world that is not yet under his direct kingship (1 Cor. 4:8–9).

In the same way, Christians have often spoken of the biblical teaching of the "priesthood of all believers." Again, this is qualified. Jesus is the only mediator between God and humanity (1 Tim. 2:5), and the Old Testament priesthood is now completely fulfilled in him. Someone, then, would sin grievously to sacrifice a goat on the church's communion table or to say to an unrepentant sinner that his sins are forgiven. This does not render the idea of the "priesthood" void, but defines it. In Christ, we are a kingdom of priests (1 Pet. 2:5; Rev. 1:6; 5:10).

This means that each of us, by the torn body and shed blood and active mediation of Jesus, has access to the Father, and we pray and intercede for one another before God. In Christ, all of us participate in the prophetic calling.

But in many ways this could hardly seem to be less true. Elijah, for instance, was obviously different and distinct in his life and calling, a strangeness seen even in his attire and in his diet. The same was true of his eventual successor, John the Baptist. But the distinct aspect of Elijah's life and calling was the repeated message: "And the word of the LORD came to Elijah." That's part of the dynamic at work even in the way that we first find Elijah and the other prophets before and after him. Ahab is introduced in terms of his background, his reputation. He comes to us almost like a slow train coming down a track. Elijah, on the other hand, seems to come out of nowhere. He is not identified by his bloodline or his accomplishments or his pedigree. Elijah was simply "the Tishbite" from "Tishbe in Gilead," a place no one even knows how to find on a map. But that's appropriate, because that's how the Word of God works.

The Scripture at this point seems to veer off from its previous course. "Starting at the very end of Solomon's reign, the center of gravity shifts from kings to prophets; the narrative refocuses attention away from palace intrigue and royal enterprises, including even war, as primary shapes of history," writes scholar Ellen Davis. "Rather, what comes to the fore is the sovereignty of the prophetic word itself, operating in ways that may go beyond the intentions and hopes of the prophet and sometimes run directly counter to them."[2] Elijah comes, Davis argues, "from no known lineage, from an unknown place in the hinterland, far from the centers of power," precisely because the point is not Elijah, but the Word he carries, a Word that is dangerous not only to Ahab and Jezebel but to Elijah too.[3]

Here's what this has to do with you in your struggle against fear. Just as there is a priesthood of all believers, there is also a prophethood of all believers. Jesus said that John the Baptist was in the spirit of Elijah, and that John was the greatest prophet up until that point. And yet, Jesus also said, startlingly, that "the one who is least in the kingdom of heaven is greater than he" (Matt. 11:11). On the Day of Pentecost, Peter said that the coming of the Spirit was in fulfillment of the words of Joel: "And in the last days it shall be, God declares, that I will pour out my Spirit on all flesh, and your sons and daughters shall prophesy" (Acts 2:17). This has happened. And the preacher of Pentecost, Simon Peter, later in the Bible explained how and why.

Peter spent a great deal of time establishing that he was an eyewitness to the life and teachings and resurrection appearances of Jesus. He also, though, was an eyewitness to an Elijah sighting. Once, remember, on a mountain, Peter and his two companions saw Elijah with Moses, transfigured in light with Jesus (Matt. 17:1–13). To the churches, Peter recounted this, along with his testimony that he, personally, had heard the voice of God thundering out in response to this strange event (2 Pet. 1:16–18). And yet, Peter does not choose this as his claim to uniqueness in history. Instead, Peter wrote, in contrast with that eyewitness event: "And we have the prophetic word more fully confirmed, to which you will do well to pay attention as to a lamp shining in a dark place, until the day dawns and the morning star rises in your hearts, knowing this first of all, that no prophecy of Scripture comes from someone's own interpretation. For no prophecy was ever produced by the will of man, but men spoke from God as they were carried along by the Holy Spirit" (2 Pet. 1:19–21).

"There are no proofs for the existence of the God of Abraham. There are only witnesses," wrote the late rabbi Abraham Joshua Heschel. "The greatness of the prophet lies not only in the ideas he expressed, but also in the moments he experienced. The prophet is a witness, and his words a testimony."[4] More than the miraculous and supernatural things his eyes had seen, Peter spoke of the prophetic word as the foundation of his witness. In the Scriptures, we have the "prophetic word," the revelation of God. And through the Scriptures, we all are witnesses to the truth of the gospel, a witness we are then directed to carry into all of the world (Matt. 28:19). This is still true.

The word of the Lord came to Elijah, and, in Christ, the word of the Lord has come to you.

This revelation is a matter of integrity. And, again, despite the way we use the word *integrity* primarily in terms of the character (mostly) of other people, the underlying metaphor of the idea of integrity is architectural. A building has "integrity" when its construction is sound, when it can hold together. Jesus used this metaphor in his familiar parable of the two houses, one built on solid rock and the other on sinking sand. The first could withstand the storms and winds, but the second collapsed—and, as Jesus spoke, "great was the fall of it" (Matt. 7:24–27). That's a story about integrity. And notice that it works in two ways, both the outside and the inside. On the outside, the "rock" that gave support in Jesus' story was the Word of God. On the inside, the life built upon something else might have looked impressive and sturdy but ultimately collapsed in on itself. And we see this theme again in Jesus' words about the temple. Jesus was decidedly unimpressed with the structural integrity of the temple in Jerusalem. When his disciples were gushing about its magnificence, Jesus said, "Truly, I say to you, there will not be left here one stone upon another that will not be thrown down" (Matt. 24:2). But the temple that Jesus is constructing of, as Peter would put it, "living stones" (1 Pet. 2:4–8) cannot be shaken, because it is built on a word from God.

What this has to do with courage is clearly seen in the trajectory Elijah took away from Jezebel. We know the *why* of that flight into the wilderness ("Elijah was afraid"), but we should also pay attention to the *where*. The prophet was not, after all, wandering aimlessly. He was headed somewhere, to Horeb, "the mount of God" (1 Kings 19:8). One would be forgiven for passing right over this detail, as just another geographical note that only is of interest to people who pay attention to the maps at the backs of their Bibles. But Horeb is no mere detail. We've seen this mountain before. Moses went there when he too was frightened by the threat of arrest by authorities. And while there, Moses encountered God in a bush that burned with an unearthly fire (Exod. 3:1–5). Later in the Moses story, the fire would fall again, as from there God delivered through Moses his commandments for the people of Israel.

This was the mountain from which the Israelites had started out their journey into the promised land (Exod. 33:6; Deut. 1:1–6). And Elijah here was following this path backward, setting off through the wild back to where the people had heard from God in the first place. The question is: Why? And that's why we must go back to Elijah's initial statement to Ahab, "As the LORD lives, before whom I stand." The language here is, as we noted earlier, accountability before the Judgment Seat of God, but it also is language of integrity.

Elijah defined himself as one accountable for the message he delivered. He was one who would stand by his words. And now, here he was—his zeal burned out in crisis. His world in that moment didn't seem to hold together. So Elijah went back to the starting-point, not just of his own story, but of the story of his people. To have courage one must have integrity, and to have integrity one must have some sense of what can be depended on, of what word one can trust.

And in order to see this we must realize just why the kings and the prophets were so often at odds with one another. Both offices (along with the priesthood) were necessary for the integrity of the people of God, but in very different ways. Some observers of popular culture will point out the ways that fictional characters in books or films or games can often be divided up into agents of order or agents of chaos, as those who maintain stability or as those who disrupt stability. In a very real sense, that distinction makes sense of the divide between the kingly and the prophetic (even apart from the sewer-level immorality of Ahab and Jezebel).

The kings were to maintain order and continuity. Even though, by the time of Elijah, the kingdom of Israel had "dis-integrated" into two kingdoms with two thrones, the kingship was still rooted in the line of David. That's why the royal genealogies were important. To ask where the king was, one must only point to the royal family, and that's where the next king would be as well, and the one after that. But this stability, when left alone, decayed often into royal presumption. The institutions, over time, came to see themselves as self-generating and self-supporting, just as God predicted they would (1 Sam. 8:10–18). And, as virtually every earthly power everywhere has concluded, nothing can better secure power than control over what is defined as truth, or at least, what is allowed to be spoken of as truth.

When the prophetic is under the control of power, rather than the other way around, the results are cover-up and manip-ulation. Think of Balaam, for instance, commanded by the king to use blessing and cursing as military strategy or the endless numbers of court prophets, who would offer a word the king wanted to hear, in exchange for their personal safety or financial security or just proximity to power. The Law of Moses, though, laid out the requirement that the king was to write out a copy of the Scriptures, to read them every day (Deut. 17:14–20), to remind him who he was and to whom he was accountable. God knew that a king would have the tendency to mistake himself, as Pharaoh of Egypt had, with a god.

And so, God would send prophets, whether Samuel to Saul, Nathan to David, or Elijah to Ahab, reminding all these author-ities that none of them were authorized to manufacture their own truth. The prophets reiterated a message Martin Luther conveyed in hymn-form, "That word above all earthly powers, no thanks to them, abideth." In this way, God introduced to the stability of the kingship the chaos of the prophetic word. The kingship was designed to maintain order and continuity, while the prophetic was meant to provoke crisis and disruption. Both were necessary for integrity, for things to hold together. The Word of God had integrity even when the institutions did not.

This dynamic is still at work. Look no further than the way truth and authority are used in the cover-ups of physical, sexual, and spiritual abuse in church contexts around the world—often by an established and respected spiritual authority, often through quoted Bible verses, and all in order to prey on innocent victims. And, when caught, they almost always defend themselves by appealing to some perverted concept of grace. "God can forgive anything," we're told by abusers who appeal to such as justification for remaining in their positions of authority, while retaining access to future victims. Likewise, they almost always compare themselves with King David in Psalm 51. But in so doing, they co-opt the Bible, and even the gospel itself (or, rather, a cheap, unbiblical version of it) as cover for their crimes.

The New Testament warns us that often "wolves" are present to introduce false doctrine, but, just as often, these spiritual carnivores hold to orthodox doctrine, at least on the surface, in order to use it for predatory ends, just as the sons of Eli used the biblically-directed sacrificial system to collect fat for their consumption and to lay with women at the altar (1 Sam. 2:12–22). Virtually every New Testament letter warns us about the same phenomenon (2 Pet. 2; Jude). Why would this be the case when there's so much opportunity for debauchery out there in the world? Why, in other words, would a predator seek out a spiritual environment? The answer is vulnerability. Spiritual predators target these environments in order to exploit the weak and vulnerable. And to do so, they take on all of the requisite behaviors of committed believers. A skilled predator can mimic discipleship when he is just "casing the joint," watching the mores, learning the phrases, mimicking the convictions. Such people often use authority, even quoted Scripture, to the point of identity theft. These wolves are drawn to innocence and trust the way a vampire is to human blood.

But even in far less awful circumstances, power seeks to co-opt God's words for its own ends. Ahab was born to be king, and Jezebel to be queen, but, in a very real sense, so were you. Humanity, after all, was created to serve as image-bearing rulers, under God, over the cosmos (Gen. 1:27). But that rule was to be directed by God's word, a word that the Serpent twisted and distorted ("Has God really said?") in order to take these rulers captive to its own reign (Gen. 3). The Scripture confronts the kingdoms we set up in our own lives, redirecting those kingdoms to its purposes. And yet, the temptation is always to shape the Word of God into a court prophet, saying to us exactly what we want to hear.

But a Word-based integrity points us to a truth outside of us, unalterable by our interests. In almost every culture, people have had stories of shamanic experiences based on the reciting of a secret word or a mysterious code, in spells or incantations. This idea shows up in all sorts of folklore and cultic practices. But why? Could it be that the underlying pattern—the connection between Word and reality—is what is being redirected and plagiarized here? Jesus encountered many shamanic attempts to channel power through word. The demonic beings tried—and failed—to use Jesus' name in order to get power over him (Mark 1:24). Jesus instead drove them away with his own word (Mark 1:25), sometimes by asking the piercing question, "What is your name?" (Mark 5:9). Moreover, in teaching us to pray, Jesus disentangled us from the notion that magic words or vain repetitions were needed to get God's attention (Matt. 6:7). We come to God in Jesus' name, not as some disconnected, impersonal talisman, but because we are actually united to Jesus.

Our words matter because the Word matters. And the Word matters because all of the created universe around us is originated and sustained by a Word (John 1:1), not an impersonal word that can be channeled and manipulated but a Word that has become flesh and dwelled among us (John 1:14). In the Scriptures, then, we are addressed by a living Word of God, which becomes a lamp unto our feet and a light unto our path. And, by the Spirit, then, we cry out the words "Abba, Father!" and "Jesus is Lord!" Elijah was returning to Horeb because Elijah understood that the integrity of his God was bound up in the integrity of his Word. And he was right. More than that, everything depends on the integrity of that Word.

While much about the universe is a mystery to us—and that mystery grows the more we learn about physics and other natural sciences—we could not even speculate or seek out the workings of the universe if it did not have integrity, at least some coherent soundness holding everything together. In a biblical vision of reality, that coherence is not, ultimately, a thing, such as the laws of mathematics or of logic, but a Person. The *Logos* of God is the One "by whom and through whom" everything was made, and that Word became flesh and dwelt among us (John 1:1–2, 14). Of this person—the Lord Jesus Christ—the apostle Paul wrote, "For by him all things were created, in heaven and on earth, visible and invisible, whether thrones or dominions or rulers or authorities—all things were created through him and for him. And he is before all things, and in him all things hold together" (Col. 1:16–17).

In Christ Jesus, heaven and earth are joined together, and in union with him a fractured humanity is summed up in one "new man," pictured already in the church reconciled to God and to one another through him. When looking at the vast cosmic sweep of creation, Paul said that the mystery of God's purposes is summed up "in Christ as a plan for the fullness of time, to unite all things in him, things in heaven and things on earth" (Eph. 1:9–10). No matter how chaotic or random the universe seems, it really is an ordered cosmos because it is ordered around and through and in the person of Jesus Christ. The revealed Word of God points us to him, and then, by the Spirit, "re-integrates" our lives around him.

We must recognize that virtually anything created by God can be twisted to dark purposes by the world, the flesh, and the Devil. That includes obedience to authority. Social psychologist Stanley Milgram plumbed one aspect of this with experiments he conducted, revealing that people would commit acts they would think immoral or unethical, as long as the responsibility was diffused to the group or to a commanding figure rather than to themselves. "A substantial proportion of people do what they are told to do, irrespective of the content of the act and without limitations of conscience, so long as they perceive that the command comes from a legitimate authority."[5] This corruption extends in innumerable directions, "religion," in many ways, being a primary example.

In our current context, many say that they object to the insistence of Christians, and others, that truth is objective and non-relative. Now, to some degree, what people rightly object to is the way some Christians seem arrogant in their own perceptions of the truth, when the Scripture itself tells us to maintain humility since we "see in a mirror dimly" (1 Cor. 13:12). But, in reality, what many more people object to about Christians is not, in fact, that we hold too strongly to the reality of a truth external to us, but that we don't hold to that at all.

I think often of talking to a Roman Catholic parishioner about the sexual abuse revelations that were coming out about churches in both his and my respective communions. He disclosed to me that he was considering stopping his weekly attendance at Mass. "It's not because I doubt that what my church teaches is true," he said. "It's that I doubt whether my church believes that what my church teaches is true." The suspicion this man had is that "truth" in his context was a handmaiden to power, rather than the other way around. Now, regardless of whether that is true in his case, it is a question that refuses to go away, because the stakes are too high.

Often one will hear denunciations from religious people of individualistic "do-it-yourself" spirituality, the kind that defines itself as "spiritual but not religious." And, of course, there is much to critique, with all sorts of cultural influences that lead to this sort of churchless and gospel-reductionist spirituality. But perhaps Western secularizing and individualizing culture is not all that is to blame. Perhaps religions themselves bear responsibility too, in ways that are too often left unexamined.

Political scientist Eitan Hersh, as he criticizes "political hobbyism" among people of his ideological tribe, notes a similar dynamic at work in religion. Noting the many abuses of power by clergy, Hersh theorizes that many people are intentionally seeking religions that are "deliberately powerless," which "rejects the power of community and thereby avoids getting burned."[6] This, of course, does not achieve its goal—as any examination of all the ways lightly organized cults and gurus also abuse their power, but the dynamic should prompt religious communities to ask what about us drives so many to search for these deliberately powerless spiritualities. Maybe, for many, it is exactly what we say it is—the modern drive to autonomy, but perhaps for many others the rejection is not of the sort of community described by Jesus but the predatory and rapacious institutions that have harmed them, all in Jesus' name.

In Alan Moore and Dave Gibbons's 1980s-era graphic novel *Watchmen*, a central aspect of the plot is the plan by evil genius Adrian Veidt to fake an attack on New York by a psychic alien squid, resulting in the real death of half of the city's people. The reason for his manipulative plan was to force the United States and the Soviet Union to back away from their imminent nuclear Armageddon, by uniting them against a common threat.[7] Now, obviously, we are not quite to the point of squid attacks, but often "truth" is mobilized for similar purposes.

When I began teaching seminary students, I was startled to see how many of them knew theology, but only in terms of current controversies. To some extent, of course, this has always been the case. Error forces the church, as in the Christological and Trinitarian debates of the first few centuries of the church, to clarify what is believed. But with some of these students this seemed less to me about seeking clarity through controversy as much as it seemed to be the thrill of marking out whose side one was on in a fight. Some people even seemed bored by biblical or doctrinal or practical truths that couldn't be marshaled in debates against others. This is the spirit of the age.

No matter where one is on the ideological or religious spectrum, one is expected to use certain language, to assent to certain "facts," and to be willing to discard those facts and convictions as soon as they become less useful to one's "side" than to the other side. The "truth" is an aspect of power, meant to shore up unity against a common foe. As with the *Watchmen* universe, though, this unity is short-lived. Once people realize they have been motivated by what is not true, the result is a burned-over concoction of cynicism, nihilism, and simmering rage—along with paralyzing fear.

Consider the ways that global cultures, and even your own psyche, have been altered by the rise of a constantly morphing social media infrastructure. We all know that these platforms amplify the voices of what are sometimes called "trolls," those extraordinarily wounded souls who seek out such venues to vent their inner demons with anger. But researchers have noted that these platforms don't just provide venues for these "trolls," but are also making virtually every one of us influenced by these media a little more "trollish." To show why this is, technology expert Jason Lanier compares human nature to that of wolves, arguing that in every human personality there is the mode of the solitary and that of the pack.

When our "switch" is set to "pack," he contends, we shift into emergency mode, to the protection of the real or imagined tribe from threat. This mode is necessary, he argues, because we can all think of times when individuality should essentially evaporate into the larger collective. On the largest scale possible, imagine if a nuclear bomb (or a giant alien squid) were to drop right now onto Times Square in New York. The country would need to rally together, almost as one organism, to deal with the emergency and to fight what would no doubt be a war of unimagined proportions. This is true on a much smaller scale as well. Your family Thanksgiving table might be occupied with all sorts of debates and disagreements, but if these are interrupted by a telephone call saying that a nephew has been critically injured in a car accident, the family will need to merge into a kind of collective. But these times should be rare, Lanier argues, and the "switch" should usually be kept in the "solitary wolf" mode.

"When the Solitary/Pack switch is set to Pack, we become obsessed with and controlled by a pecking order," Lanier writes. "We pounce on those below us, lest we be demoted, and we do our best to flatter and snipe at those above us at the same time. Our peers flicker between 'ally' and 'enemy' so quickly that we cannot perceive them as individuals. They become archetypes from a comic book. The only constant basis of friendship is shared antagonism toward other packs."[8] This is why, Lanier argues, nonsense is a more useful tool for spreading "viral" content than is reason or imagination or truth. When "truth" is defined by what is useful for building group identity, one's embrace of that "truth" is a signal not that it is based in reality but instead that it is what makes us part of the "pack." This is accelerated by modern forms of media but predates all of them. This can happen in a family, in a church, in a workplace, and usually it does not happen by overt pressure to say one believes what is not true, but rather through a kind of self-censorship, of just not thinking about uncomfortable questions that might put one out of the "in-group." Often these powers don't so much demand that one lie to others as that one lie to oneself.

The novelist Marilynne Robinson wrote, "A society is moving toward dangerous ground when loyalty to the truth is seen as disloyalty to some supposedly higher interest."[9] That's especially true when loyalty to the truth is seen as disloyalty to a tribe. This can happen in any human conscience, in any family, in any workplace, in any church. The truth can be conformed to whatever the power structures are, rather than the other way around. When this happens, integrity is in crisis.

For years many have warned about "moral relativism," about the dangers of an eclipse of objective morality. These warnings were right, and are seen now almost everywhere, including in the rhetoric of some who spent a lifetime warning about moral relativism. Notice how, inside and outside the church, people are loudly denunciatory of the evil behavior of their political, religious, or cultural opponents, and yet, when the same thing is true of their allies, they are muted or even attempt justifications for the behavior. Whenever this is the case, you can be sure that these people don't believe in morality or truth or justice, but in their allies. They believe in power. They believe in themselves. That's not the way of Christ.

We should not cover over dangerous injustice out of some desire to protect "the cause," whatever that cause is. The way of Christ does not advance by deceit or by hypocrisy, but by bearing witness to the truth—even when that truth is ugly. If you make apologies for predatory behavior because the predator is "one of us," then you are not standing for truth, and you are potentially sacrificing countless other lives, no matter what you tell yourself. And sometimes this is the way some of the most heated controversies work. Heated issues are bandied about by whatever means—regardless of how false the facts behind them turn out to be. The point is not the truth of the arguments, but only how those arguments are used to prove whose side the various parties are on, and to bolster the togetherness of the group.

In reality, though, such a lack of integrity is not difficult to see for those who are on the outside. Consider, for instance, the widespread distortion of Christianity, exported from America all around the world, in the so-called "prosperity gospel." These heretical preachers promise health and wealth and well-being to those who will complete the transaction of praying a prayer (and, usually giving money to the preachers), despite the fact that this is the opposite of what Jesus and his apostles taught, at every point. This "gospel" travels all around the world damning souls and picking pockets at the same time. Despite that, these purveyors of what the apostles would have called "a different gospel" are welcomed as fellow evangelicals by many who purport to hold to the gospel, even as these same people anathematize those who disagree with them on political alliances or cultural strategies. This is the natural result of an American Christianity that often equates "bigness" with truth, again the very opposite of what Jesus and his apostles taught.

In evangelicalism—a church reform movement supposedly committed to Scripture as the sole ultimate norming authority—biblical illiteracy abounds, with slogans and memes replacing the narrative and teaching of the Bible, often even by those who say they are committed to biblical inerrancy and exposition. In a populist movement based on crowd support, it is much easier to find out what one's "base" already believes and add Bible verses to that than it is to shape and form consciences over decades with the Word of God. The world can see this for what it is.

As Eudora Welty observed, the noise of the crowd—any crowd—pretends that it is about whatever the "issue" is being debated, but rarely is. Instead, she wrote, this noise is "the simple assertion of self, the great, mindless, general self." And that is ephemeral, she argued, because it lacks meaning, and only meaning lasts. "Nothing was ever learned in a crowd, from a crowd, or by addressing or trying to please a crowd."[10]

An entire generation is watching what goes on under the name of American religion, wondering if there is something real to it, or if it is just another useful tool to herd people, to elect allies, to make money. Is Christianity really about the crucified Christ, they ask, or is it about ethnic superiority claims or wacky televised conspiracy theories or political sloganeering? One need not spend much time on a college campus or among previously churched young adults to see why many of them have rejected what calls itself "Christianity"—and, sadly, they leave aside not only these cynical distortions but also the gospel itself.

For those of us who believe in Truth with a capital "J" (Eph. 4:21), this is a matter of worship. For those of us who believe in the doctrine of hell, this has eternal consequences. You can only hold together, long term, if one knows that there is more to life than what you are making up, or what someone is making up for you, in order to help you make it through the night.

This sort of integrity, though, is not just about the external truth—the words over Mount Horeb or the authoritative text breathed out in Scripture. It's about the integrity of the message, but also the integrity of the messengers. Novelist, essayist, and poet Wendell Berry said that one factor leading to the disintegration of communities and persons is a loss of those willing to "stand by their words," which he defined as including both *fidelity* and *sincerity*. That means that one recognizes a truthful authority outside of one's own manipulations and that one is willing to be accountable for that word, to have one's life conformed to it. This means, in short, standing by one's words and having words that can be stood by.[11] When, earlier, Elijah had prayed for the resurrection of a widow's son, a death she blamed on the prophet himself, the son returned to life. The widow's response is instructive: "Now I know that you are a man of God, and that the word of the LORD in your mouth is truth" (1 Kings 17:24). Both parts of that sentence are important. And they are just as important in our time and place, as they were in the ancient Middle East. The Word of God is not dependent on the integrity of the vessels bearing it, and that's good news.

I remember how shaken I was the first time a preacher I admired was shown to have been living a double life as a serial adulterer. I wish that feeling had gone away, but it showed back up when I saw others I admired revealed to have just as much a double life albeit with raging tempers or emotionally abusive marriages or habitual lying instead of sexual sin. Maybe that's happened to you with someone who maybe baptized you or helped you through a deep depression, and you may wonder if this means that everything you learned from that person is as fraudulent as he or she turned out to be. Not necessarily. There were, without doubt, people in the first century who heard the gospel first from Judas Iscariot. After his treachery and then suicide, these people may have wondered if their own faith was a sham. But what they responded to, if they responded in faith, was not to Judas but to the message he delivered, and that message stands regardless of the motives of the messenger (Phil. 1:15–18).

But this does not mean that the integrity of the witnesses to the Word is of no importance. As a matter of fact, Jesus said that the world would see the authenticity—the integrity—of his message on the basis of the love his followers would have for one another (John 13:35), and the lack of this sort of authenticity leads to the nations reviling God himself (Rom. 2:24). Moreover, Jesus castigated the ways the religious leaders of his day pointed to a truthful revelation—the Word given by God to Moses at Horeb—with lives that were, privately, at variance with that Word (Matt. 23:2; Mark 7:11–12). That's entirely consistent with the prophets of old who said the same about the worship of God's people being rejected because their lives demonstrated that they didn't believe the words they were mouthing (Isa. 1:12–17). This is an ongoing crisis, in every era.

For example, a study in recent years on the use of pornography by conservative evangelical Christian men found a key difference between their interaction with the sexual content and that of the outside world, namely, that the Christian men simultaneously morally rejected and personally consumed pornography. This was described by the researcher as a persistent state of "moral incongruence" between what these men thought they believed and how they lived their lives.[12]

The language of "congruence" is appropriate. In describing the respect he had for the integrity of a person he admired, Eugene Peterson defined that man's life as one of "congruence," by which he meant, "no slippage between what he was saying and the way he was living." He wrote, "The Christian life is the lifelong practice of attending to the details of congruence—congruence between the ends and the means, congruence between what we do and the way we do it, congruence between what is written in Scripture and our living out what is written, congruence between a ship and its prow, congruence between preaching and living, congruence between the sermon and what is lived in the preacher and the congregation, the congruence of the Word made flesh in Jesus with what is lived in our flesh."[13] This congruence is not achieved in this life, but the congruence is aspired to, and is where the Spirit leads. That's because the congruence is not to an abstract moral code or to a set of principles, but to a particular life—to the life of Christ himself.

God's objective for us is that we be "conformed to the image of his Son, in order that he might be the firstborn of many brothers" (Rom. 8:29). That has everything to do with the courage to live out one's life and calling.

This sort of congruence is harder than it sounds. Jesus commanded us to let our "yes be yes" and our "no be no," or, in other words, to work to see that our words are congruent with our intentions and thoughts. Reflecting on the moral harm that happened to his native Czechoslovakia under Communist domination, dissident playwright (and later president) Vaclav Havel wrote, "We fell morally ill because we became used to saying something different from what we thought."[14] In this case, this incongruence between speech and thought was largely the result of external threat—the authorities and the secret police were watching for any signs of rebellion so people learned to talk in ways that parroted what was expected of them. For most people, though, the loss of congruence happens in a more willing participation in our loss of integrity.

That's because the pressure to conform manifests itself not just in what we would think of as overt pressure. As one legal scholar explains it, much of what we pick up from other people are cues about "what you ought to do and say if you want to remain in their good graces."[15] The result does not feel, most of the time, like what we would recognize as hypocrisy. "Even if you disagree with them in your heart of hearts, you might silence yourself or even agree with them in their presence," this scholar writes, referencing whatever crowd is pressing the individual to conform. "Once you do that, you might find yourself starting to shift internally. You might begin to act and even to think as they do."[16]

Sociologist Peter Berger noticed this dynamic at work back during the debates over racial segregation in the Jim Crow South. Many have noticed how many white pastors and leaders—even those who would have conceded privately that they knew racism to be wrong—said nothing or even sided with the forces of white supremacy. Why did this happen? Berger demonstrated that those churches with pastors who took "unpopular" stances on this injustice suffered immediately in the arenas of "success" (numbers of members and finances). Those who were in a membership drive (and who isn't?) or a building program could not help but know what the "cost" would be to talk about such matters.

Berger argued that in many cases it was not that these ministers lost a conflict with racist parishioners as much as that they sought to avoid conflict by essentially "talking themselves into" the views of the majority around them. "Ministers then may be perfectly sincere when they maintain that they have always acted in accordance with their conscience," Berger wrote. "The social forces of the situation have already taken care that this conscience will be so formed as to remain innocuous."[17]

This form of "social religion" conditioning the pulpit indicated a crisis for Christianity itself. "If God is truth, He will not leave alone the one who passionately desires truth," he wrote. "In the end, Christian truth and human integrity cannot be contradictory."[18]

Sadly, this crisis of a socially-conditioned conscience, even in the pulpit, did not disappear with the desegregation of schools and lunch counters, but persists to this day. Indeed, this crisis exists in some form or other in every generation, since it is right at the heart of what Jesus himself warned us about: "Watch out; beware of the leaven of the Pharisees and the leaven of Herod" (Mark 8:15). At issue was "leaven" or yeast, which Jesus had already used elsewhere as an analogy of the kingdom of God. Yeast works under the surface and invisibly. Jesus identified this "yeast" with both Herod—civic or political power or status—and "the Pharisees"—religious rule-keeping that appears to be orthodox.

Much of what emotionally mobilizes the twenty-first-century North American church is not related to Christian life or doctrine or mission, but to "Christianity" as a set of values under siege by others. Whether one is trying to conform Christianity to the dominant culture or whether one is trying to rail against that dominant culture by conforming Christianity to the tribal values of a "Christian" subculture, the end result is the same: exhaustion. It's hard to keep up with all the compromises one is called upon to make.

After all, the values one would need to affirm in order to be "one of us" this year might be irrelevant the next year. The cultural degradations one would denounce, loudly, right along with the rest of the herd in one year would become acceptable in the next, just depending on the personalities and the pet sins and injustices of one's "side" at the moment. What would be characterized as watching the wall of righteousness in one year might well be deemed self-righteousness or moral elitism in another. And, through all of that, there will always be people who will pay attention. No matter how you attempt to tell yourself, and others, that you are committed to truth and to authority, those who bother to watch those inconsistencies over time will see that what you had was never conviction but ambition. And in your deepest psyche you will see that too. That sort of life is not just artificial and inauthentic, but also exhausting.

Good Friday is on the Christian calendar as an ongoing warning of the persistent temptation toward illusory power. After all, the cross happened at the endpoint of a series of decisions, the endpoint of a series of compromises of integrity, at the endpoint of a series of quests for political status. Herod wanted to demonstrate loyalty to Caesar. Pilate didn't want to risk popular disapproval. Many of the people wanted Barabbas, a resistance leader who would fight instead of one whose kingdom was "not of this world." The Roman state dressed Jesus in a fake "kingly" costume in order to make fun of him. Onlookers ridiculed Jesus' appeal to his Father, sure that he was cursed by God and thus lacking any power at all. And yet, in the moment of humiliation and weakness and isolation, the cross revealed the power and wisdom of God. The Darwinian struggle to see who is fittest, who is more threatening or more impressive is, then and now, a way that leads to death. It's the way of the cross that leads home.

Right before God withdrew into silence for four hundred years, before the coming of Christ, he spoke through the prophet Malachi, once again joining Elijah and Horeb. "Remember the law of my servant Moses, the statutes and rules that I commanded him at Horeb for all Israel," God said. "Behold, I will send you Elijah the prophet before the great and awesome day of the LORD comes. And he will turn the hearts of fathers to their children and the hearts of children to their fathers" (Mal. 4:4–6). In other words, God, in the end, will conform the integrity of his people to the integrity of his Word. And that happens through a cataclysmic crisis.

That crisis doesn't stay off in the future though. It has come to you in Christ. So how do you find integrity? Part of it happens through the slow, gradual process of a life lived in discipline to the Word of God. But often, as with Elijah, integrity is created not by how well you "hold yourself together," but through the reverse—through a breakdown of the sort Elijah faced on his way to the mountain.

In the past, people would often speak of people having "a nervous breakdown." This language could refer to everything from a psychotic break to a midlife crisis to a bad day, which is why it is so rarely used today. But there's something about the lingo of "breakdown" that is grounded in something real. The difference though between those who "stand" in courage and those who "fall" into cowardice is not that one faces breakdown and the other does not. At a certain point in almost any life, one comes to see that things one once saw as solid are being shaken apart. This can be good news.

Your integrity is formed by habits, put together over years and decades, but God often breaks through all that habituating and performing with a moment of crisis—with a "breakdown" of sorts, if you will—in order to show us that we stand not on our own strength but by grace. In these moments God is doing for us what he did for his people as he delivered them from Egypt, bringing them right to the moment of what seemed to be hopelessness, when they despaired of their own ability to navigate the situation before saying, through Moses, "Fear not, stand firm, and see the salvation of the LORD, which he will work for you today. For the Egyptians whom you see today, you shall never see again. The LORD will fight for you, and you have only to be silent" (Exod. 14:13–14). Even those outside of the faith have noticed something of this experience: namely the need to find courage in a place that is, as one leadership expert puts it, "beyond hope and fear."[19] This means giving up the expectation of predicting visible outcomes based on one's own skill and simply stepping forward for the task to be done. One management consultant describes these times as "the neutral zone," in which people look back and realize that though they didn't know what was happening at the time, their lives were being redirected toward a transition.[20]

This often feels like an ending—like the giving up on a dream—when in reality it is often the breaking apart of a numbness to things to which one should pay careful attention, pointing the way forward. What, in fact, is happening is a breaking down of the status quo. If we don't experience such moments, we can never find genuine integrity or genuine courage because we will root these things where they cannot actually "hold together" at all, in self-reliance and self-sufficiency.

What we can see here is something akin to the phenomenon experts see when they study "resilient" and seemingly invulnerable children, who deal with difficult circumstances well. Often these super-resilient children fall apart in midlife. The child actually needed to grapple with the crises of childhood—not just to hide behind people-pleasing or performing for a demanding parent—in order to navigate the crises coming later on.[21] Integrity is not a matter of "holding it together," but of breaking down in the right way—and then standing back up.

In the wilderness, God was conforming Elijah's life to his words. He will do the same for you and for me. And he does that by causing us to find our integrity not in our willing and doing, but in the truth by which we stand. In the end, it doesn't matter if you are named for Elijah, or for Jezebel. The truth is outside of you, and able to conform your life to that truth, so long as you don't insist on conforming the truth to your life instead.

Our integrity can only come through a breaking down of who we thought we were, a shaking up of what we thought we knew. We are the patients, not the doctors. And the chart in our hands is our own.

God help us.

Chapter Five

# Courage and
# Vulnerability

## *Power through Weakness*

E ncountering the god of thunder on a subway train does
not happen every day, so when it did I took notice. What
piqued my interest was the large tattoo on the arm of the tired-
looking, rail-thin man sitting next to me. The image was of a
hammer, surrounded by lightning, an image I thought I recognized as Mjolnir, the hammer of the Norse thunder-god Thor.

I assumed this man was a fan of the character Thor, transi-
tioned from Norse mythology for the comic book medium over
fifty years ago by the late Stan Lee. Thor the superhero had
gained even more traction in popular culture in recent years

due to a successful string of film adaptations of the character. Though I normally don't strike up conversations in such settings, this time I did, asking the man if he was a fan of Thor. He said that the tattoo was indeed of Mjolnir, but seemed perturbed that I would equate it with the Thor of fantasy book and film. "It's my religion," he said.

Now, of course, I was truly intrigued so I asked some more. The man said that he was part of a small group of neo-pagans across the world who seek to revive the worship of the ancient gods. Thor was, for him, his favorite of these beings. I asked further what it was about Thor that he found compelling. Using saltier language than I should convey here, the man explained that Thor did not take any pushing around from anyone. "Our religion is not a religion of weakness," he said. "Thor is about strength and power. He's a winner." I thought for a moment and said, "I don't suppose there could be anything more opposite from Thor's hammer than Christ's cross." He looked back at me and replied, "Exactly. That's the point."

I spent the rest of the day trying to imagine this man's life. Despite his tattoo, he certainly did not appear to be particularly strong or intimidating. As a matter of fact, I would be willing to guarantee, just given the way he would avoid eye contact and look around nervously, that he was the kind of person who had been bullied as a teenager or as a child. This religion of his is probably not anything he experienced as part of any kind of community. There probably is no "Church of Asgard" in his town, meeting every Thursday. Instead, he most likely found his neo-pagan "community" by connecting with random fellow-worshippers through technology, maybe even as part of one of the white supremacist organizations seeking to find mascots in the old gods. He didn't look like a faith-threatening pagan to me, just like a scared kid. And that's probably why he was drawn to Thor.

The god's power, he could imagine, could be channeled through him, like magical lightning through a hammer. Thor's hammer could crush his fear, he might have supposed, and the crashing of thunder could drown out the sounds that scared him in the night. In that sense, this young man was not all that different from most people. And, even in his rejection of Christianity, he seemed to understand more about the cross than even many Christians do. He saw right away what the entire world of the first-century Roman Empire recognized as the scandal of Jesus: he was crucified. That meant he was defeated by his enemies. He was dominated by the Empire. That is no way for a god to act, no way for a hero to act, no way even for a courageous mortal to act. And, as the stranger on the subway car might put it, that's the point.

I couldn't help but think, as I walked away from the train, about Jesus right after his triumphal entry into Jerusalem. "Now is my soul troubled," Jesus said, "and what shall I say?

'Father, save me from this hour?' But for this purpose I have come to this hour. Father, glorify your name" (John 12:27–28). What is striking about this is that Jesus was expressing what sounds like anxiety about his future, even as he recommitted himself to carrying out that mission.

This is the same Jesus who was the most decaffeinated figure in the Gospels—the man who remained calm as the disciples panicked over their ship nearly capsizing, and appeared so nonchalant as the crowds demanded food when only scraps were available. This was the same Jesus who taught his followers to be "anxious for nothing," and not to be afraid. And yet, here, Jesus is troubled at the core of his soul.

But as Jesus cried out in this anguish, he spoke of his defeat of the ruler of this age, of his own power as that of one who is "lifted up from the earth," imagery that pointed not to his fame or strength but to his coming crucifixion (John 12:32–33). And this idea was disturbing to all of those around. He was, after all, supposed to be the Messiah, the delivering king, who is supposed to be around forever. But, as Jesus spoke of this hour of powerlessness approaching, God affirmed it with his own voice from the skies. The crowds, though claiming to long to hear a word from their God, could not understand such a word in this context, in the context of a cross of weakness.

"The crowd that stood there and heard it said that it had thundered," John recounts (John 12:29). They managed their own fear by convincing one another, and themselves, that the sound they heard was just a natural phenomenon. No doubt one person said to the person next to him, "Did you hear that? That was just thunder, wasn't it?" Thunder was an interesting choice, of course, because thunder and lightning are among the most awe-inspiring aspects of the natural order. They bring with them what's necessary for life and well-being, rain for the crops, and they strike fear with their potential for mortal danger, with their reminder that nature gives life, but nature can also kill. From earliest times, human beings identified storms as being messages from the gods. Here the people translated a message from God into just a storm.

Thor, of course, was not the first storm-god. These myths differ in many ways, but a common theme that holds them all together is power. A god of the storm is a god who is mighty enough to defend against any enemy or threat, and a god of the storm is able to give the rain needed for prosperity. It's little wonder then that in places as culturally and geographically different as Norway and Nigeria, Polynesia and Mesopotamia, these thunder-gods were almost always around. The world of ancient Israel was no different. Baal was the god of the storms, of the rain, of the night sky filled with thunder and lightning. His consort Asherah was a goddess of fertility. Appeasing these gods with worship was necessary, it was believed, to keep food on the table and to keep horrible things from happening.

Anyone who has ever lived through a famine (not most of us) can understand this sort of fear about the future, and anyone who has ever huddled in a basement during a tornado or walked across an open field as the sky cracked with lightning can understand this sort of terror of mortal danger. Baal and Asherah were bulwarks against such fears. Baal was power, and one could harness that power for oneself. Beyond that, though, the very presence of Baal in Israel at this time was the result of a quest for power. They were, after all, in the land of Israel, probably first of all because of their political and diplomatic utility. The marriage of Ahab and Jezebel created a delicate détente among nations that could have threatened one another.

The merging of Jezebel's old-country gods with Ahab's inheritance from his Israelite forebears was probably not so much the "Let's find the truth in all religions" sort of religious pluralism that we often encounter today as much as a fusing of the two backgrounds of the king and the queen for the purpose of consolidating political power. Moreover, Baalism was a folk religion—a religion that could harness the power of the people by keeping them unified behind the king. And Baal was about power.

Before the wilderness crisis, Elijah appears to be a figure of power and strength, too. After all, he is driven out of the country not because he displayed too little power, but too much. He had humiliated Baal. First, he did so by withholding rain, demonstrating that a storm god who couldn't bring rain was an impotent failure, even on his own terms. Then, of course, there was Mount Carmel. Baal was supposed to be responsive to incantations, so that his power could be harnessed by those who claimed to speak for him. And yet, there on the mountain, he was silent, did nothing, seemed to not even pay attention to the cries of his gatekeepers. God, on the other hand, responded immediately to Elijah's word, sending down fire on the water-soaked altar Elijah had built. Not only was God vindicated, but so was Elijah, his sarcastic taunting of Baal ending up verified. Elijah showed that, when it counted, the god of rain and thunder was dry and silent. That's a repudiation. And then Elijah took on the priests of Baal, and uprooted all of them. In so doing, Elijah not only humiliated the mythical god, but also the very real king. I don't know how many of you have ever worked alongside a truly malignant narcissist, but, if so, you will recognize the response here immediately. This type of person is repulsed by any suggestion that he or she might be weak or ineffectual. When humiliated this type of person will react with rage—sometimes a "hot" temper-tantrum sort of rage, and sometimes a "cool" icy sort of score-settling. Jezebel, humiliated, seeks to reassert her power with a dead prophet.

And then things changed for Elijah. Elijah was full of zeal, and full of strength. He was, despite being outmanned and outgunned by the crowds and the throne, winning. That is why he was confused to find himself, gasping for air and his zeal burned out, on the run in the wilderness. God was doing in the prophet at Mount Horeb what he had done through the prophet at Mount Carmel: he was uprooting idols and revealing himself.

God was showing Elijah something, first of all, about Elijah himself. The story emphasizes that Elijah was hungry and thirsty. He arrived at his destination, Mount Horeb, after having been without food and water for forty days and forty nights (1 Kings 19:8). He did not die, though, only because he had been cared for—given food and water by an angelic stranger there in the desert, who told him that such nutrition and hydration would be necessary "for the journey is too great for you" (1 Kings 19:7). Again, this crisis in the wilderness was not the first time Elijah had experienced this sort of provision, but was an intensification of ways God had already been at work.

After announcing the drought, for instance, Elijah survived because God directed him to a brook for water, and ravens brought food to him (1 Kings 17:4). In this, God was, it seems, combining what we might think of as "ordinary" and "extraordinary" means of provision. One might come across a brook, and conclude that this is just a coincidence. Rarely do we think much about from where our every drink of water comes. The ravens, though, are extraordinary. And in their feeding of Elijah, he is reminded of his relative powerlessness. Ravens, after all, are a scavenging bird—the sort that did not return back to

Noah after the flood because of the carrion on which they could feed (Gen. 8:7). A raven was unclean, forbidden to any Israelite to eat (Deut. 14:14), and yet they were feeding the prophet. Elijah was, apart from God, a dead man.

Moreover, the ravens feeding Elijah were part of an entire cosmic web of provision, since God is the one who feeds the ravens. God made that point to Job, in pointing out the mystery and awe of the created order, "Who provides for the raven its prey, when its young ones cry to God for help, and wander about for lack of food?" (Job 38:41). And, in the fullness of time, Jesus would tie our own provision to that of the ravens. While most of us remember more Jesus' line "Consider the sparrows," from Matthew's Gospel, Luke records Jesus as saying, "Consider the ravens: they neither sow nor reap, they have neither storehouse nor barn, and yet God feeds them" (Luke 12:24). Jesus was warning against anxiety, teaching us that we can trust God. Elijah was learning not only that God cared for the ravens, but that he was dependent for his life on that fact. Elijah was shown, by his need for food and water, that he couldn't take anything for granted. And then in the various ways God had fed and watered Elijah—birds, a vulnerable widow, now a stranger on the side of the path—God was caring for Elijah apart from anything he could will or work or do. Elijah had to see that he was a creature, not a machine or a god.

And in all of that, God was intervening. He was keeping Elijah from becoming himself an Ahab. The central problem for Ahab and Jezebel, and the idolatrous rulers who came before and after them, was not, first of all, that they worshipped idols (though that would be bad enough), but that they made an idol of themselves. The images and the cult of the Canaanite deities were a manifestation of the fact that the royal house believed they were exempt from the commands of God. Their cavalier announcements of having arbitrary power of life and death further showed this. Ahab and Jezebel sought to root out dissenters, those who "trouble Israel" by speaking of things as they really are. They used the levers of state and cult to rob a vulnerable poorer man of his family inheritance for their own appetite for more.

The tendency here is exactly the same as the prophet Ezekiel would denounce in the prince of Tyre who believed himself to be a god and not a man, an illusion God rendered ridiculous in his death (Ezek. 28:1–10). Likewise, in the New Testament, Herod Agrippa found himself flattered by people (also from Tyre and Sidon) because their country depended on his for food. They shouted, for instance, after he delivered a speech, "The voice of a god, and not of a man!" But an angel struck him down, Luke recounts, "because he did not give God the glory, and he was eaten by worms and breathed his last" (Acts 12:22–23). This is not just a kingly temptation.

All of us, at the top of our strength, face the danger of thinking that this strength is unlimited and self-derived. For those who do not belong to God, often that delusion continues until death shows them, too late, that they are not, in the end, the "winners" they thought they were. For those who belong to God, though, God sees to it that we recognize our creatureliness, and how dependent we are on God for our life and breath and being. That's part of what God was doing for Elijah in that wilderness.

That's why the storyline of Elijah in 1 Kings is filled with narrative clues pointing the hearers and readers back to another story. Elijah is making the exodus trip backward, through the Jordan toward Horeb, and, having been fed and hydrated in remarkable ways by God he walks "forty days and forty nights" (1 Kings 19:8). The Israelites of old, while wandering in their own wilderness, had encountered both extreme hunger—such that they grumbled that they would have been better off back in Egypt where at least they were fed—and then feeding from God. This provision from God showed up for them both in what they would have considered "ordinary ways"—they might not have noticed had God not pointed out that their clothing, and even their own feet, did not wear out on them during forty years of wandering (Deut. 8:4)—and in what could only be described as miraculous, manna appearing from the heavens (Deut. 8:3).

All of this though, both the hunger and the provision, was for the purpose of God discipling his people, toward a specific end: "that he might make you know that man does not live by bread alone, but man lives by every word that comes from the mouth of the LORD" (Deut. 8:3). This was necessary, God revealed, because of the future of this people, they would be coming into a land of blessing. God would "do you good in the end," but the danger would be that the people would conclude, "My power and the might of my hand have gotten me this wealth" (Deut. 8:16–17). That Israel had forgotten this part of their story is obvious in their complicity, as a whole, with the fertility religion Ahab had given them. God saw to it, though, that Elijah would not.

In this provision in the wilderness, God demonstrated not only that Elijah must not act like Ahab, but that God is nothing like Baal. Yes, both were thought necessary for rain, for crops, for fertility, but God was not, and is not, a prosperity idol. He was no means to an end. Notice the way that the worshippers of Baal appealed to him on Mount Carmel. They cried out to him from morning until noon, "O Baal, answer us!" (1 Kings 18:26). After Elijah taunted them, due to the silence with which their pleas were met, they "cried aloud and cut themselves after their custom with swords and lances, until the blood gushed out upon them" (1 Kings 18:28). They raved on and on, the text says, but "there was no voice. No one answered; no one paid attention" (1 Kings 18:29). The god of provision was seen to be repudiated, on his own terms.

A great deal of this, though, is precisely because of the function Baal played; it was not a transcendent Being but a tool. They thought they could get this deity's attention with the loudness of their yelling or with the frenzy of their dancing or even with the shedding of their own blood, since he was as transactional as they were. This is exactly what Jesus warned against, when he said not to approach God with "empty phrases" (or as the KJV reads, "vain repetitions"), as the nations of the world do, "for they think that they will be heard for their many words" (Matt. 6:7). Instead, Jesus taught his followers to speak to God as a Father, one who already knows what we need even before we do, and to appeal simply, "Give us this day our daily bread" (Matt. 6:11).

This is precisely the difference between Elijah and the prophets of Baal, the difference between Elijah and the royal house. Again, the temptation we might have is to view the pyrotechnics of the life of Elijah in such a way as to think of him as almost another species from us. But this is not the case. As a matter of fact, Jesus' brother James wrote to the first-century churches that they should see not how different Elijah is from us, but how much the same. "Elijah was a man with a nature like ours, and he prayed fervently that it might not rain, and for three years and six months it did not rain on the earth," James wrote. "Then he prayed again, and heaven gave rain, and the earth bore its fruit" (James 5:17–18). We have precisely the same access to the "power" of Elijah that he had, and that's because he had no power on his own at all. He had prayer, an appeal to God for provision and for deliverance. And so do you.

But just like us, Elijah was also prone to forget that he could count on this, no matter how many times or how many ways—through blackbirds, through a foreign widow, through an angel by the side of the path—that God had provided for him. Even in this, though, we see the difference between God and Baal. God is not subservient to his prophets, as though his actions were contingent upon some secret means of manipulation. If God were, in fact, the "God of Elijah" in that sense, then Elijah would have died when he appealed to God for death. God stands in total contrast to Baal, in both his working and in the worship he demands. And this, of course, is all about power.

Defining God in terms of power leads precisely to the sort of mentality found in the folk religion of Baal. And this mentality did not die out when fire was called down from heaven but is alive and well today, albeit under different names. That's one of the reasons I've argued for years that the so-called "prosperity gospel" is not a branch of historic Christianity, nor is it is a new religious movement. The prosperity gospel is a revival movement—reviving ancient Canaanite fertility worship. This is not the gospel of Jesus Christ, but witchcraft.

The "prosperity gospel" is a pyramid scheme—in both the Pharaoh-era Egyptian and modern marketing senses of the word—and the charlatans who peddle it count on those who are seen as in the line of historic Christianity to vouch for them, so that they can tear apart more and more lives. Many are willing to do just that, in exchange for the carnal benefits, including large numbers and political mobilization, that such a coalition of lunatics and heretics can supply. The end result is more cynicism for those who are not completely desperate or gullible, and hell for those who fall prey. That sort of "Christianity" is the way of Ahab and Jezebel, not of Jesus and Elijah, and ends up in the same place that Ahab and Jezebel did, discredited, dismantled, and lapped up by dogs.

And yet, this tendency not only belongs to those who seek to fleece the unsuspecting of their money or their votes, with Jesus as the unquestioned and unquestionable mascot, but is the ever-present temptation of every single one of us, to turn our God into a transactional being with whom we can bargain: "I promise I will read my Bible every day, if you will let this pregnancy test come back positive" (or negative, as the case may be) or "I will never yell at my children again, if you will just let me get promoted to foreman." This is not who the God of Jesus Christ is, and that is good news for all of us. Sooner or later, after all, whatever "impressiveness" we believe we have to offer to the world, or to God, will falter. And then who are we?

Elijah there in the wilderness lamented the fact that his zeal—listed off in the litany of what he had done and what had been done to him—ended in failure, and therefore he was deserving of nothing but death. In order to stand before God, he must be recreated, once again, with a renewed sense of gospel power.

This is necessary for all of us. The apostle Paul faced a barrage of accusations against him from detractors in the first-century churches. They first feared Paul because he was too strong—he was the "zealous" Pharisee who was on his way to murder the churches. But then, after his way of life as an apostle was seen, the accusations changed; Paul was not too strong but weak and ineffectual, not at all impressive in his speech or presence. In light of all of this, Paul refused to dwell on his unusual mystical experiences with God, but instead highlighted the ways he had been consistently defeated—run out of town, imprisoned, shipwrecked, abandoned, betrayed, opposed, even plagued with a mysterious "thorn in the flesh" that God would not remove. But Paul testified that God had said to him: "My grace is sufficient for you, for my power is made perfect in weakness" (2 Cor. 12:9). For Paul, this reframed his very definition of power and of success: "Therefore I will boast all the more gladly of my weaknesses, so that the power of Christ may rest upon me. For the sake of Christ, then, I am content with weaknesses, insults, hardships, persecutions, and calamities. For when I am weak, then I am strong" (2 Cor. 12:9–10). While most Christians know these words, or at least recognize them, we rarely see the radical reorientation bound up in them.

When I was a teenager, I was a rule-following "good kid" who never was in any trouble at school, except for one time, when I was accused of cheating. Math was always my worst subject, and geometry was an ongoing nightmare for me. My teacher asked me to stay after class, to question me about a cryptic code he had found on my final examination, right below my name, the letters "ICDATTCWSM." I blushed, horrified to even be accused of being a cheater, and then blushed even more as I explained that this wasn't a code unlocking the answers to the test (and I couldn't even imagine how a jumble of letters could do that) but was just a mental reminder to myself. They stood for, "I can do all things through Christ which strengtheneth me," from the King James Version (the only version I knew existed) of Philippians 4:13. As I look back on it, though, I realize that I had no idea what this verse actually meant.

Paul was not writing that Christ was a source of power that one could tap in order to succeed or prosper, but instead was arguing just the reverse. "Not that I am speaking of being in need, for I have learned in whatever situation I am to be content," he wrote, "I know how to be brought low, and I know how to abound. In any and every circumstance, I have learned the secret of facing plenty and hunger, abundance and need. I can do all things through him who strengthens me" (Phil. 4:11–13).

The real application of this verse is not that, with Jesus on my side, I can do it—I can pass the test—but, rather, "In Christ, I know how to live as either one who passes this test or as one who fails it, as one who is on the honor roll or as one who is grounded by my parents, as one who graduates high school or as one who is a dropout, as a winner or as a loser."

This is important for courage because, while many would say that a key to working up courage is to think positively about oneself and one's abilities and the future, studies have shown that more often the reverse is true. Pessimism does not necessarily lead to an Eeyore-like curmudgeonly cloudiness, but instead to a reframing of what one's expectations are. If I do not expect utopia, I realize that I can live through what I fear. I can survive—not by denying the reality in front of me but by allowing it to point me, through my weakness and desperation, to the God who knows what I need. That means that I serve a God who will not grant me everything I want (Elijah prayed to be dead, remember), because he is more on my side than I am. And part of what I need is the sort of reliance on him that can only come through joining Jesus in the suffering of carrying a cross.

That's why Paul reframed suffering in the opening of this letter to the Corinthians. His suffering, he wrote, was not random or meaningless but was instead a participation in the sufferings of Jesus himself (2 Cor. 1:5). And these sufferings were the reason that Paul could then comfort others as they suffered

(2 Cor. 1:6–7). Haven't you noticed the way that God continues to do this? When my wife and I were grieving through infertility and miscarriage, the people who could most care for us were those who had suffered in the same way. The most effective women I know at ministering to pregnant women in crisis are those who lived through the same situation. How many cancer survivors, or those who have lost loved ones to cancer, are the ones given the gift to minister in oncology units or hospital waiting rooms?

One of the pastors I revere the most is one who was fired from not just one but two wealthy suburban congregations, and then ended up planting a church that started tiny in a rented room in a city and grew large ministering to people who were hurting, many of them misfits in American religion. I heard this pastor say to his congregation, "Think back to the time in your life when you were the worst failure, the time of which you are the most ashamed. Jesus was not absent from you then, embarrassed by you then. That is the place and the time where Jesus is holding you the most gently." And, as he said it, he had the credibility of one who did not just know this truth but who had embodied it in his own life.

The interplay of God's provision and God's deprivation is meant to pry our hands away from the prosperity idols to which we are all drawn. "For we do not want you to be unaware, brothers, of the affliction we experienced in Asia," Paul wrote.

"For we were so utterly burdened beyond our strength that we despaired of life itself. Indeed, we felt that we had received the sentence of death. But that was to make us rely not on ourselves but on God who raises the dead. He delivered us from such a deadly peril, and he will deliver us. On him we have set our hope that he will deliver us again" (2 Cor. 1:8–10). These words are astounding. All of us—no matter how strong or how successful—are all headed for ultimate failure. After all, as the economist John Maynard Keynes once said, "In the long-run we are all dead."

At some point, you will lie in a bed, gasping for air. And, at some point, you will see the heart monitor beside you bouncing all over the screen. There won't be a thing you can do about it. All you can do is to rely on a power outside of yourself, a power found in a crucified and resurrected Christ, who alone can lift you out of the grave and into a new creation. Your own resources will not be enough. Between now and then, God is preparing you for that moment. He does so by giving you what you need, and he does this by making you feel your need, to make you hunger and thirst for the righteousness that can never come from you.

In redefining the messenger, God also redefines for us the message itself. Elijah certainly exhibited the language Paul used above, one who was once under a sentence of death, at the end of his own resources. But it is where God led him that caused him to see more clearly exactly what the power of God is, and what it is not. The Bible tells us: "And behold, the LORD passed by, and a great and strong wind tore the mountains and broke in pieces the rocks before the LORD, but the LORD was not in the wind. And after the wind an earthquake, but the LORD was not in the earthquake. And after the earthquake a fire, but the LORD was not in the fire. And after the fire the sound of a low whisper" (1 Kings 19:11–13). Only after all of this did Elijah come to the mouth of the cave for his climactic encounter with his God.

This passage is easily misunderstood, especially the mention of what some translators render as "the sound of thinnest silence." What is the sound of silence? This seems at first glance almost like a Zen Buddhist koan along the order of "the sound of one hand clapping." This is further complicated by the way some Bible translators have sought to make sense of this seeming contradiction by rendering the event, a "still, small voice" that comes after the tumult of the quakes and fires and thunders. This has led to many people concluding that the way to hear from God is through the "still small voice" in their hearts.

In Peter De Vries's novel *The Blood of the Lamb*, the narrator reflects on sitting through a sermon on this section of Scripture: "We agreed we had heard too many sermons on this verse, which was supposedly calculated to disarm prolonged and complex exposition."[1] One can certainly see the frustration expressed there, as the narrator sums it up: "Well, anybody who talks for forty-five minutes on the value of silent meditation . . ." And yet, perhaps there is a good reason why Christians are drawn so often to this text, to try to encounter with words an experience of standing in awe without words, and of finding God there.

Now, certainly, wisdom does not come simply through the explicit process of reasoning. Much of what it means to grow in wisdom and holiness means the cultivation of certain affections and inclinations, that may, at times, feel like a "gut-level" response. But, as with our reasoning, these intuitions are fallible. As I look back on my life, there are all sorts of times I wish I had listened to my "gut" telling me things such as, "These people are crazy," when, it turned out, they were. But my still, small voice, I have learned, tends to hate all the same people I want to hate, and to revel in the same sorts of sins I want to commit. Your internal "still, small voice" can be as deceitful as any other part of you, and just might lead you to fight and fornicate all the way to ruin. But that's not what this means.

As a matter of fact, the text does not say that God was in the thin silence, only that the silence was the punctuation before God spoke to Elijah. This was, remember, the very same place where God, speaking from a burning bush, had met Moses. In that event, God was present in his creation but was distant from it—the bush was afire but not consumed. And when Moses asked for his name, God replied, "I am that which I am." A similar dynamic is at work here. God revealed himself to Elijah, but the first word that had to be said was that he was not Baal. Some have suggested that Israel's Lord being outside of nature is the "supremely important concept for the tribes of Yahweh."[2] The fact that God was not "in" these manifestations of nature on the mountain made clear to Elijah that a relationship with God would not be, as in these earth religions, the harnessing of God's power for human ends.

If the only aspect of God Elijah had ever seen was the Mount Carmel fire-fall, he would be tempted to make God into just that kind of being too—a way to vindicate himself and to humiliate his enemies. But God reveals to him much more. God would speak, of course, on his own timetable. First, though, Elijah would stand before him in silence. Thus, having beheld that awesome spectacle, of whirlwind and earthquake and fire, Elijah endured those moments of quiet. And after all of that tumult, and then all of that silence, God resumed right back with what he had been saying before: "What are you doing here, Elijah?"

Unlike at Mount Carmel, where God allowed himself to be called down from heaven by his prophet, here he is the one doing the calling: "What are you doing here, Elijah?" In doing this, God was speaking not with power as defined by Baal—brute domination—but with an entirely different sort of power, with *authority*. Lord Jonathan Sacks, one of the world's most respected rabbis, wrote years ago of the way that power can become corrupt in the relationship between men and women, with men using physical or financial or cultural strength to dominate and mistreat women. This is not just injustice (although it is certainly that) the rabbi taught, but is rooted in Baalism. "Baal," after all, means "master." But as God revealed to Hosea, his people were not to call him "Baal," but "my husband."[3]

The difference could not be starker: "For Hosea, at the core of Baal worship is the primitive idea that God rules the world by force, as husbands rule families in societies where power determines the structures of relationships," the rabbi writes. "Against this Hosea paints quite a different possibility, of a relationship between marriage partners built on love and mutual loyalty. God is not *Baal*, he-who-rules-by-force, but *Ish*, He-who-relates-in-love, the very word Adam used when he first saw Eve." The difference between authority and domination is key. They are not the same thing, by any means.

God was demonstrating his uniqueness from prosperity folk-religion. He was speaking with authority, and not as one of the Baals. This distinction is important because as sociologist Robert Nisbet pointed out, "power" is defined by coercion based on raw force coming from the outside, while "authority" is rooted in allegiance and communion. One might also say "covenant." Nisbet wrote that, "Power arises only when authority breaks down."[4] Suppose you were attending a wedding, and you notice in the program: "Out of respect for this happy occasion, the parents of the bride ask you to please stand during the bridal procession." Likely, in fact, this would not even be spelled out. People in a given community would just know, "This is what we do at this part of a wedding," and, if not, they would stand as they saw others around them doing so. That's a very different thing than your reading in the bulletin, "Stand when the bride walks down the aisle or armed guards, who are watching you, will break your legs." This is coercion and force, rooted in fear, not authority rooted in belonging and allegiance.

One of the strangest things about the figure of Jesus of Nazareth in the Gospels is just this. As Mark writes, "And they were astonished at his teaching, for he taught them as one who had authority, and not as the scribes" (Mark 1:22). This authority is demonstrated all over the pages of the Gospels. Jesus speaks to demons, and they flee. He speaks to the wind and the waves, and they are still. He speaks to his followers, simply saying, "Follow me," and they drop their nets or their government-issued moneybags or their revolutionary weaponry, and just do it. This was remarkable because what drew them to Jesus was not their fear of retribution from him, nor was it their hopes to gain anything in worldly terms from him. His authority was grounded in his own personal credibility, in the drawing and transforming power of his own voice.

This is still the case. The apostle Paul explained how it is that all of us went from the dominion of darkness to the kingdom of God, and it was precisely the same way he did: "For God, who said, 'Let light shine out of darkness,' has shone in our hearts to give the light of the knowledge of the glory of God in the face of Jesus Christ" (2 Cor. 4:6). That kind of authority is strikingly different from Pharaoh-like or Ahab-like or Baal-like appeals to authority rooted in coercion and domination. That's why authoritarian systems—whether churches or governments or families—ultimately reveal simmering resentments underneath. That's because there was no real authority there, but just the suppression of what people really felt and thought, for fear that they would be punished or exiled.

Baal was not just an idol, but a government program. Jezebel is the source of this idolatry we are told, bringing these gods with her from the old country. It is not likely that Ahab commanded their worship because he loved Baal and Asherah, or because he thought that they loved him. Likely, this was, like perhaps the marriage itself, a way of consolidating power, of shoring up the political alliance. And the end result was a folk religion, a religion that could "unify the people," and keep them from, well, "troubling Israel."

I fundamentally disagree with Karl Marx on just about every aspect of his understanding of God, the world, history, economics, morality, and so on, but there's at least one thing he was partially right about. Religion can indeed be used as an "opiate" of the people, to numb them from seeing what is happening around them.

I would argue, further, that religion can also be used as a "cocaine" of the people, revving them up to mobilize on behalf of whatever the powers-that-be deem useful. Even as I write this, the totalitarian government in China is seeking to uproot religions, whether Christian or Muslim or Buddhist, that relativize the power of the state, while seeking to incentivize forms of religion—including domesticated forms of ancestor worship and even tepid versions of Christianity—that they can use to build national identity and bolster the authority of the dictatorship. Caesar always seeks to do away with those who would serve "another king, Jesus" (Acts 17:7) but rarely minds those religions that will proclaim "Jesus (or whomever)-and-Caesar Are Lord."

We can see the way our various gods and idols are marshaled against one another in the constant anger of our age. Rarely do I pay much attention to car bumper stickers, but I think about one of them all the time, and I'm not even sure that I understand what it means. A journalist sent me a picture of the sticker, attached to a car next to hers in a post office parking lot somewhere. The message read, "If Jesus Had a Gun, He'd Still Be Alive Today." When I saw it, I shook my head and mumbled, "Jesus *is* still alive today."

At first, I assumed the car belonged to a professing Christian, probably an evangelical like me, making a point about his or her views on gun ownership. That's what angered me, but not because of the viewpoint. I'm no pacifist, and I think there is a place for Caesar to wield the sword against evildoers (Rom. 13:1–7) and for people to defend their imperiled neighbors from harm. What angered me was instead that Jesus here was just a means to an end, a way of punctuating a viewpoint one would already hold, and doing so in a way that was itself biblically illiterate. Such examples are not uncommon. But in this case, to even make that point one has to sacrifice, literally, the integrating point of the entire Bible.

To me, that's precisely what's wrong with religion as a useful tool for anything—political success, economic well-being, personal status, or anything else. The peril here—even on matters in which one is right—is the use of God as a tool. This is nothing less than a repudiation of who he is as God. "The people who would make of God an ideological weapon in our political conflicts are engaged in blasphemy," wrote sociologist Peter Berger a generation ago, and that blasphemy, he rightly perceived, is in contradiction with what God, through his prophets, revealed repeatedly about himself. "The God of the prophetic message stands sovereignly above all nations and empires," Berger wrote. "He cannot be invoked as a safe political ally—even by Israel."[5]

The more I thought about the bumper sticker, though, the more I considered that it might not belong to a Christian at all, but instead might be a secularist making fun of our politicized American Christianity or a gun control advocate making fun of gun-rights activists. Or, I thought, it could even belong to an outright neo-pagan, like my Thor-worshipping seatmate, making fun, just as the old pagans did, of Jesus himself, as a weakling who could not even defend himself from attack. I still don't know. But it really doesn't matter, because, at the core, any of these messages boil down to the same thing—an understanding of power as assertiveness and aggression and winning.

A stupid bumper sticker is a stupid bumper sticker. And I wouldn't even mention it if it weren't that the message contained there is so often the majority report, even among those who profess the gospel. The idea is that Jesus would not have been victimized if he had only had the power to defend himself. And yet, that assertion is what Jesus repeatedly refuted. No one took his life, he said; he willingly laid it down (John 10:17–18). The apostle Peter agreed with the sentiment of this bumper sticker, taking a sword to the head of the guard attempting to arrest Jesus. The result? Jesus rebuffed his disciple. Who needs a sword when one could call twelve legions of angels (Matt. 26:47–56)?

Jesus was not overwhelmed by someone else's power. He was showing us what power is—the power of the cross that seems weak to the world. Indeed, Jesus told Peter that the power he sought to hold back his enemies would ultimately consume him (Matt. 26:52).

More importantly, Jesus knew what the real crisis was, and is. The crisis was not the threat of external harm. The crisis was a world under the just condemnation of God. The resolution of this crisis could not come from human effort, but from the sacrifice of the Lamb of God. Peter thought his biggest enemy was the Roman Empire. Jesus could see past the Roman Empire, to Satan falling like lightning from heaven. In a time of the idolatry of winning and displaying, we can often tell what we really care about by what ignites our passions, what drives up our blood pressure. And, in our time, those are usually not about the mission of the gospel but about the identity politics of seeing "our side" as better than some other group.

In those debates, what is being defended is not Christ and the gospel but "Christians," sociologically or culturally or politically defined. Again, we can see this in what drives us to lament or anger. Our ancestors of old were enraged by the loss of their land and their temple to foreign conquerors, but weren't angered at all by their own placing of idols within the temple of God (Ezek. 8:1–18). Jesus, on the other hand, was not triggered by the all-consuming passions of the arguments around him—whether one should pay taxes to Caesar, whether one should side with the tax collectors or the zealots, with the Pharisees or the Sadducees. He certainly wasn't angered by his own treatment from those around him. And yet, he was visibly enraged by those who would wall off the temple or the Bible from those seeking God (Matt. 21:12–17; 23:1–36).

Our cultural and moral and policy debates are important. Offering one's opinion is good, sometimes even necessary. But if our passions demonstrate that these things are most important to us, are central to our identity, then we have veered into a place we should not go. That's why North American Christianity is sick and weak, and doesn't even know it. We are bored by what the Bible reveals as mysterious and glorious, and red-in-the-face about what hardly matters in the broad sweep of eternity. And why? We clamor for the kind of power the world can recognize, while ignoring the very power of God that comes through Christ and him crucified. We trade away the Sermon on the Mount for influence and access because the Sermon on the Mount seems weak and surrendering. And through it all we demonstrate what we really care about—the same power and self-leverage this age already values. We think if only we were more aggressive and dominant and powerful then we might not be victimized. We might win, like Thor, instead of lose, like Jesus.

But power is not found in the way of domination but in the way of crucifixion. That claim is breathtaking in its audacity. The crucifixion—the execution of a criminal, thought to be a shame to the community, a defeated foe of the state, and under the curse of God—was the last thing a religious movement seeking an audience in the first-century Roman Empire would emphasize. As a matter of fact, even acknowledging it would seem to be conceding the argument to "the other side." Crucifixion, after all, was a clear sign of Rome's power. A line of crosses on a roadside was a warning to anyone who might think of challenging the powers-that-be. The cross is, Paul taught, a scandal—to everyone—once we really understand it, because it upends our understanding of power and wisdom and success and winning. How different this is from the pose of power we often aspire to, or pretend to have achieved. Paul wrote that he proclaimed only Christ and him crucified because "the foolishness of God is wiser than men, and the weakness of God is stronger than men" (1 Cor. 1:25). In fact, Paul contended, "God chose what is low and despised in the world, even things that are not, to bring to nothing things that are, so that no human being might boast in the presence of God" (1 Cor. 1:28–29). Strength is found not in the path of glory but on the road to Golgotha. And that's precisely where God was leading Elijah—to the cross.

Now, most of us do not aspire to power in the sense of a super-villain in a lair, laughing maniacally about plans to rule the world. But all of us, left to ourselves, seek to define ourselves in this social Darwinian context of winning and displaying. Sometimes this sort of domination-hunger is obvious to those around a person, though usually not to the person himself or herself. Most people, of course, don't have, as Jezebel did, the authority or the will to maintain power over the life and death of an individual, but they can use their power in other ways. A person can threaten to withhold his tithe or escrow his offerings if a church doesn't go along with his way. If he gives a lot of money, he can use that "power" as mighty leverage, the way a primate might seek to establish dominance through physical aggression in the wild. Someone else might gossip in a workplace in order to keep a rival from getting a promotion, or at least to seed enough doubt about that person to make it less likely.

You might believe yourself to be exempt from this because you are perhaps reluctant to seek attention, and maybe averse to arguing with anyone else, but you are not. All of us must overcome this pull, even when it is seen not in quarrelsomeness and dictation but just in the quest to be seen as impressive and put together.

I once found myself talking to an older, much wiser man about some of the most painful times of my life. "Did you notice, Russell," he said, "that when you would talk about these painful things, that you would smile?" I had not, in fact, noticed that, but he was right. Somewhere along the way I had learned that appearing vulnerable would be to appear weak, would invite more attack, and so I smiled my way through it all. I can see that pattern all over my life, at almost every stage of life. The constant smiling, the waving off of any problems mentioned to me, was not a reflection of reality but a Darwinian survival strategy.

Now, no matter how much people may ask you to be "vulnerable" and "authentic" with them, you do not owe everyone—even within the church—access to all of your hurts and pains and struggles. God has given different sorts of friendships and relationships to us for a reason. Still, most of what we are expected to do in our era is spin control rather than mutual burden-bearing. We want to appear strong—and sometimes "happiness" is part of that strength—precisely for the reasons a lizard puffing itself up to look bigger does, to ward off threats. That's about power, but it's a skewed vision of power. The way of Jesus calls us to stand up for others in their hurt, but to be willing for ourselves to be reviled or misunderstood or even pitied by people who think we are "losers."

But we don't want to follow this way, because, like Simon Peter, we all seem to know that this way doesn't work. And our intuitions here are right. The path of the cruciform life does not, in fact, "work" if we judge it by the standards of success that have enveloped us since birth. If you don't "hit back" with a devastating comment to an insult, you are at a disadvantage, with everyone else who does. If you won't gather groups around to say "Everyone is concerned about . . ." to get your way in a congregational decision-making session, you are at a disadvantage before those who will. If you forgive those who have hurt you, you might be hurt by someone else again. All that's true. In the short-run, eye-for-an-eye Darwinism produces much better results than Sermon-on-the-Mount Christianity.

God repeatedly demonstrated, in the lives of his people, that his way toward power comes in a different way than that of the fallen world. That is why he called Gideon to pare his army down to a relatively tiny band of men. That is why he forbade the Israelites from choosing a king based on physical impressiveness. That is why he denounced those who would seek their safety in alliances with the might of the Egyptians, rather than in seemingly powerless dependence on God. And this way continues all the way to our present reality. The revelation of Jesus to John—unveiling the mystery behind what is seen—contrasts the power of "the Beast" with that of a Lamb. The Beast comes with might and prowess, complete with court prophets who will say, "Who is like the beast, and who can fight against it?" (Rev. 13:4). Those who are ruling, though, are those who ought to be pitied—those who had their heads cut off by the Empire

(Rev. 20:4). Babylon is impressive and powerful, and its future is a fall. Jerusalem is beleaguered and defeated, and yet the New Jerusalem will stand forever.

In the short run, in almost any arena—home, work, church, state, culture—feats of strength make better sense than carrying a cross. But that's the short run, and life is a vapor. Our ultimate problem is that we are held captive to an alien power, the god of this age, to the tyranny of our own appetites, and to the inevitability of our own deaths. Against that, folk religion will do nothing. Against that, power-posturing is useless. Against that, "success" is just more of the same.

The crisis of Elijah was, on its own, nothing at all, worthy only, as Elijah himself wanted, of being forgotten. But it pointed beyond itself to another crisis—not on the mount of Horeb but the hill of Golgotha. There Jesus was not just executed by the governing authorities but ridiculed by them (the purple robes, the crown of thorns, the "King of the Jews" sign over his head). There Jesus thirsted and was attended to by the unlikely source of the soldiers who were crucifying him. There Jesus, standing in the place of a sinful world, buckled under the curse of sin and death.

This weakness was the evidence his opponents needed that he was on the other side of God. God, after all, would not let his anointed servant suffer like this, fail like this. He screamed to the skies, "My God, my God, why have you forsaken me!"

And he was met with only the sound of thinnest silence. As he cried in Aramaic, "Eloi, Eloi, lema sabachthani?" the jeering crowds assumed he was calling for Elijah (Mark 15:34–35). He wasn't. But, centuries before, Elijah had cried out in desolation and in anguish, waiting to be heard from God. The deliverance he sought, though, would not fully come until that moment of even greater weakness than Elijah had ever known—the cross. Jesus on the scaffold was not calling out for Elijah; but instead Elijah in the wilderness was crying out for Jesus.

Courage must confront the contradiction of the cross, or our "courage" is just a better-branded kind of fear. In reality, all the ways we seek to leverage power are, just as they were for the worshippers of Baal, ways to find security from fear. To use power to keep bad things from happening to us, and to scare off anyone who might hurt us. The end result of that, though, is more fear. As the author David Foster Wallace presciently told a group of graduates: "Worship power—you will feel weak and afraid, and you will need ever more power over others to keep the fear at bay."[6] If your idol is power, you will become like that idol, and, ultimately, you will find that every idol crumbles in the end. When the idols start to topple, we will be initially terrified, and feel exposed before what scares us. In reality, we should rejoice, because we are then ready to find our way to a God who defines himself not in a gaping mouth or a grasping hand, but in a broken body and poured out blood. Once we are freed from self-protection and the clamoring for success, we are free to stand in the truth.

The German Christian martyr of the Nazi era, Dietrich Bonhoeffer wrote that "success" in the figures we aspire to be, or that we hold up as models, turns into an idolization of success that obscures even the categories of good and evil. The success itself, he argued, justifies the wrongs done. "The moral and intellectual and critical faculty is blunted," he wrote. "It is dazzled by the brilliance of the successful man and by longing in some way to share in his success." And yet, Bonhoeffer argued, "The figure of the Crucified invalidates all thought which takes success as its standard." The end result, he rightly concluded, is that the idol of success leads to loneliness and despair and, ultimately, weakness, while, "Only the crucified man is at peace with God."[7]

That's why vulnerability is necessary for courage. We need nutrition and hydration and rest. We are far more fragile than we think we are. And, though we try to avoid thinking about such things, there are moments in which we see that we are impotent before our own impending doom. Sometimes we see that in a relationship that falls apart, in a job that goes away, in a health that fails—or just in the fear that any of those things could happen. But, as with Elijah, for those who belong to Christ, there will always be a staging ground within the psyche of God versus Baal, Christ versus Mammon. God pointed

Elijah away from the way of power toward the way of the cross. And he will do so for us as well.

Our fears are not so distant from those of Elijah. Very few of us seek literal fire from heaven to destroy our enemies, but all of us seek to protect ourselves, to achieve what we define—or allow to be defined for us—as "winning." And in so doing, we put up these force-fields of self-protection around us—maybe in a sarcastic wit or in perpetual outrage or in achievement in our careers; we become not invulnerable but hyper-fragile. Baal is winning. Baal is the crowd. Baal bears the access to the crown. But God is the God of Jesus Christ, and that Christ is crucified. The sign of that cross is the power of God, and the wisdom of God, and no other way is.

The stranger on the bus next to me that day was not an enemy to be vaporized with debate. He was, like me, a sinner who is, like me, probably afraid of his own weakness. And in order to feel strong, he wants to identify himself with strength, with power, with winning. One need not resuscitate long-dead deities to do that. We all do. And we all choose our Thors and Zeuses and Baals and Dagons. But that sort of power is brittle and will ultimately fall.

Jesus is no storm-god. He bears not a hammer but nails by which he was himself hammered to a cross. That's where the real crisis is. That's why Jesus did not flinch before demons, practically yawned in the face of a shipwrecking storm, seemed nonchalant before Pilate who had the legal authority to put him to death, but then sweat drops of blood as he faced the cross. He would bear, for us, what our greatest calamity actually is: our own sin and death and condemnation. And in that sort of failure he would win. In that sort of weakness, he would overcome the world, the flesh, and the Devil. And in that sort of humiliation, God would be glorified. At least, that's what God himself said. But that was just thunder.

Wasn't it?

## Chapter Six

# Courage and Community

## *Connectedness through Loneliness*

Looking back, most of us can identify some moment in our lives we wish we could take back and do over. I have many such moments, but one of them was the time when I tried to take a country song away from some homeless men. I realize that this sounds intentionally crueler than what I was trying to do at the time, but that's what happened. I was a doctoral student, working on a degree in theology, and would spend my Monday nights once a month or so serving with some people from my church at a shelter for homeless men, downtown in the city where we lived at the time. These Monday nights featured a chapel service, and sometimes I would preach. One of the traditions at that shelter was that often the men would choose a favorite hymn to sing in the service. They chose "Me and Jesus" by Tom T. Hall. And I said no.

Now the problem was not that the music wasn't formal enough for me, a classic country music fan who could talk with those men all night long about the relative merits of the Nashville and Bakersfield Sounds. Nor was the problem for me that Hall, a revered songwriter from rural Kentucky, often sings about less than worshipful topics such as the meaning of life being summed up as faster horses, younger women, older whiskey, and more money. Again, my own personal playlists show that I have no stones to throw there. The problem wasn't even that I didn't like the song. The tune is infectious, Hall's voice perfect for it, and I would sing it often myself (though always feeling kind of guilty about doing so).

The problem was that I thought the message reinforced something deeply wrong with American Christianity, something that would show up often in the cultural religion all around me, which is the idea that religion was merely an individual matter, the person and Jesus, alone in a garden, apart from the New Testament focus on the church. As a matter of fact, I had heard many people whom I was certain wouldn't know one thing about country music, dismiss "Me and Jesus Christianity" without even realizing that they were drawing on song lyrics. But despite my reluctance, I didn't really have the pull to keep them from singing what they'd chosen. And so, minutes before I was to preach, I heard this hall full of men singing in unison: "Me and Jesus got our own thing going; Me and Jesus, got it all worked out; Me and Jesus got our own thing going; we don't need anybody to tell us how it all works out."

What I wasn't prepared for was the energy in the room, even when the first guitar chord was played, as the crowd realized what they were about to sing. Their voices were always strong when we sang something they recognized— usually old revivalist hymns about blood and grace—but when they sang this, their hands went up in the air, their eyes filled with tears, and many of them would link arms, beaming with smiles. They were experiencing community. As a matter of fact, the choice of "Me and Jesus" had been itself a community act, as they decided together among the hundred or so of them how they wished to worship. In saving them from "individualism," I had wanted to override their community, so that me and Jesus could correct their theology, and tell them how it all works out.

Over the years, I've come to realize that they hadn't misunderstood the song, but that I had. In interviews and writings, I've heard Hall talking about the writing of that song, and some of it was indeed an anthem against institutionalized religion. He said he wrote the song after hearing radio preachers manipulating people for money, putting themselves as intermediaries between God and desperate people. But he also said that the words themselves came not out of protest but out of suffering. He was repeating the words of his mother, overheard when he was a child, as she struggled to think through how to live hand-to-mouth in poverty and deprivation. "Me and Jesus will get through this," she would say.

There is a loneliness in the song, but what the men in that shelter heard was not the loneliness of the defiant contrarian, but the loneliness of one who has lost a social network of support. That was their story. Many were alcoholics. Some were drug addicts. Some grappled with mental illness. Some had committed crimes. Many of them were no longer spoken to, or even spoken about, by their families. Many of them couldn't go back to their home churches, without being ostracized and targeted with gossip and wagging heads of disapproval. That was what the song was about: "I know a man who once was a sinner; I know a man who once was a drunk; I know a man who once was a loser; He went out one day and made an altar out of a stump." When no one else was there, they could count on the fact that Jesus knew them, just as they were, and that they didn't need to come to him as part of an intact family or as a respectable member of society. He would receive them, even when they were all alone in the world.

And that's why they would almost laugh with joy as they would sing: "Jesus brought me through all of my troubles; Jesus brought me through all of my trials. Jesus brought me through all of my heartaches," and then this, the most important part, "And I know that Jesus ain't gonna forsake me now." They all knew that experience of loneliness and desperation. And, as a matter of fact, that shared loneliness was how they found community, as they joined together to make an altar out of the stumps that were left of their lives.

Few of us have ever experienced that kind of loneliness, the kind of loneliness that is mixed up not just with longing and pain, but also with fear. During his wilderness crisis, Elijah was brought right to a crucible of aloneness in the context of terror. The prophet, after all, was on the run from the royal house, but this should not be thought of merely as a fugitive outrunning a threat. In his flight from Ahab and Jezebel, Elijah was running away from his home, from the tribe of his belonging. In a certain sense, this loneliness preceded the physical isolation from his people. Elijah's identification of himself to Ahab, "As the Lord lives, before whom *I* stand," rings with the emphasis of the first-person singular because Elijah certainly appeared, at the time, to be standing alone.

Up against the prophets of Baal, Elijah was by himself against a mob, though in that moment of power he almost seems to be enjoying himself, compared to the desolation to come. Looking around there in the desert, Elijah would have had visual confirmation of his internal reality: he was indeed alone. And so he made, and then repeated to God, a lament from a lonely man: "I have been very jealous for the LORD, the God of hosts. For the people of Israel have forsaken your covenant, thrown down your altars, and killed your prophets with the sword, and I, even I only, am left, and they seek my life, to take it away" (1 Kings 19:10, 14). God's response is not what one might expect. God seems to dismiss the prophet's complaint altogether, and instead told him that he was not, in fact, alone at all. God said there was a remnant of "seven thousand in Israel, all the knees that have not bowed to Baal, and every mouth that has not kissed him" (1 Kings 19:18). The torment of Elijah's loneliness was met with a revelation that Elijah wasn't as alone as he believed himself to be.

Part of the reason this dynamic is difficult to sort out is because, if we are honest, the relationship between the individual and community is complicated for virtually all of us. Parents of adolescents will sometimes panic at the mood swings and personality changes that can come over their children. "This is not him," they might say, or, "She's not acting like our precious little baby anymore!" Sometimes, of course, there are undercurrents of serious problems present, but often there are not, just the normal tumult of those years between the shelter of childhood and the responsibilities of adulthood. In those times, people are trying to differentiate themselves from their families of origin. What really do they think and feel, and how much is just inherited from unquestioned patterns from their parents? And, at the same time, this is an age when what matters greatly is where one fits in "the tribe" of one's generational cohort. Teenagers are constantly asking, in some way or other, "What do other people think of me?" In reality, though this is heightened in adolescence, it never really goes away. In some ways, all of us spend our lives between those two dueling desires—to be an individual and to belong to a community.

At the present time, many are concerned about what is often called an "epidemic of loneliness" throughout the Western industrialized world. And this concern is valid. The skyrocketing rates of addiction, of family breakdown, and even of suicide seem to be rooted in something deeper than just economic tumult.

I can see this in my own life, even just in my neighborhood. I could map out for you, just about, the interiors of all of the houses within two miles of where I grew up. I could tell you who was related to whom, who kept candy in jars on their coffee tables, who had a secret drinking problem. And now, I am hard-pressed to tell you more than a handful of my neighbors' first and last names or what even the living room of their houses look like.

This sort of disconnection is, we assume, the endpoint of many factors—cultural forces that cause us to see ourselves as individual producers and consumers, the shifting definitions of the family, an economy requiring mobility the likes of which we have never before seen, technologies that enable us to cocoon ourselves in our own ecosystems of entertainment. And yet, along with these dizzying rates of loneliness has not come the kind of individualism we might expect. In some ways, we live in a time of heightened conformity, of a merge of individuals into the mass of tribes. Despite all of the screaming broadcast debates about political matters, very few communities, studies show, are even able to have such debates at the local coffee shop because communities tend to be "sorted" by cultural and political preferences.[1] We tend to want to group ourselves into herds where we can safely put our individual opinions in a blind trust, in order to merge into a crowd in which we can belong.

There are natural human reasons for this inclination. Years ago, I used to become fearful and alarmed by turbulence on airplanes, with my nervous system, if not my brain, concluding every time a plane started barreling up and down in the sky that the aircraft was headed for a crash. I noticed that the way I would reassure myself was by looking around at the other passengers, especially the flight attendants. They had years of experience with countless flights, I would tell myself, so if they were talking among themselves, laughing, or working through a crossword puzzle, I would relax. But if I saw a flight attendant with eyes closed, lips moving, and hands working across a set of rosary beads, I would start to get nervous.

Something about us is almost hardwired to seek safety in the herd. And yet, this sort of conformity-as-protection can have terrible consequences, far beyond that of simply a loss of individual "authenticity." One neo-Darwinian biologist noted how the loss of individuality into a herd can lead people to do things they would ordinarily never do, giving the example of Ku Klux Klan terrorists, hidden behind sheets, to all look alike, with no distinction in their faces. In any situation like this, where personal differentiation is absorbed into sameness of appearance, persons are more likely to, for instance, torture or mutilate other human beings. This is because, he argues, "responsibility is diffused by anonymity."[2]

It's not just, he contends, that the perpetrators don't want others to know who they are, but they themselves want a kind of plausible deniability, as if to say, "I didn't do this; the group did it." This biologist would never take this beyond the natural, of course, but I would argue that this reality takes us right back to the Judgment Seat, to which the human conscience points. We wish to hide from God, and often the vehicle of our hiding is behind each other, to be lost in a crowd.

This, of course, was right at the core of the Elijah crisis. He was charged with violating the unity of the people, of being a "troubler of Israel," and he was just that. The nation was meant to be united under a king—the metaphor often used was of a shepherd with sheep, and in this case, the king was evil but also powerful. Moreover, the worship of Baal itself was a driver of unity, as any folk-religion is. If community for the sake of community were the answer to the peril of the people, then God would have left Elijah in the middle of it all, untroubled and untroubling.

But God pulled him out of the mass of people, both in terms of his conviction and in terms of his ultimate physical isolation and exile. Why? Jesus identified the fear of standing alone as one of the primary aspects of cowardice. Many in the crowds hailed Jesus as the anointed of God as he entered Jerusalem on a donkey's back. But, just a matter of paragraphs later, John wrote that the root of the reluctance of the authorities to believe in him was not that they couldn't find his claims credible, but that they were afraid. Specifically, they were afraid of the gatekeepers—in this case the Pharisees—not for their physical safety but because they feared being "put out of the synagogue, for they loved the glory that comes from man more than the glory that comes from God" (John 12:42–43).

All of us, left to ourselves, have contradictory drives—to be the sole definer of our own lives and fortunes, and to meld into a hive, where we can find the visible, audible glory that we can get from one another rather than the invisible, inaudible glory that comes from God, a glory that is not seen or heard by anything but faith this side of the New Jerusalem. At the same time, Jesus was a wrecking ball to those who sought to hide behind their wealth or accomplishments or anything else. Those who came to him must embrace a Lord, and a community, one they usually would not have chosen themselves (John 15:1–16).

In addressing Elijah's fear of loneliness and exile, God pointed to a "remnant," a group of 7,000 people, unknown to Elijah, who had not "bowed the knee" or "kissed" Baal. This language is language of allegiance. That's why the Scripture says that, ultimately, "every knee will bow" to God (Rom. 14:11). This language of "remnant" is actually crucially important far beyond this episode, but is central to the larger story holding history and revelation together. This remnant of 7,000 was unknown to him—because the remnant was none of his business. As a matter of fact, knowledge of that remnant ahead of time could very well have directed Elijah somewhere other than faith. Elijah had to be reduced down to complete dependence on God, to cling to God even if he were the only one to do so. If Elijah had known all along that there was a remnant out there, from whom God would make a mighty army, he might well have put his trust in that, hidden in the "crowd" of the anti-Baal herd rather than in the "crowd" of Ahab's court prophets.

Elijah had to be alone, for a time, in order that he could serve a remnant he couldn't at the time imagine. This idea would become of supreme importance in the New Testament. The apostle Paul wrote to the church at Rome: "Do you not know what the Scripture says of Elijah, how he appeals to God against Israel? 'Lord, they have killed your prophets, they have demolished your altars, and I alone am left, and they seek my life.' But what is God's reply to him? 'I have kept for myself seven thousand men who have not bowed the kneel to Baal.' So too at the present time there is a remnant, chosen by grace" (Rom. 11:2–5). Paul's argument here is that the rejection, at the time, of the gospel by the majority of the people of Israel is no sign that God has rejected his people. Again, one should not determine questions about truth and meaning by how many people adhere to such at the moment. Instead, Paul wrote, the remnant obviously was intact; the line of faithful Israel did not end with Elijah. And, even now, God is grafting a people on to the branch of his vine of Israel. The Roman followers of Jesus were themselves the beneficiaries of that remnant of grace.

In fact, that's the way that God always works. He started the people of Israel with one man, a wayfaring stranger named Abram, and grew them into a massive kingdom. After splintering and exile and judgment, he narrowed that Israel down once more to a root out of burned ground, a tiny branch of a pruned vine, in the person of Jesus of Nazareth, who then assembled twelve "stones" who would become the foundational rocks of the New Jerusalem (Rev. 21:14). In God's purposes, the massive tree always starts with an almost invisible seed, the rushing river always starts with an almost imperceptible trickle (Ezek.

47:1–11). And the community he is forming often starts, as we have seen, in loneliness and powerlessness and irrelevance.

Elijah actually should have known that already. After the confrontation at Mount Carmel, Elijah pronounced to Ahab that the rain would start again. As Elijah bowed down before God, he sent a servant to look toward the sea, to scope out the oncoming rain. The servant came back and reported nothing, so Elijah told him to go again; still nothing. Elijah sent him again and again seven times, all with nothing in sight. The seventh time, the servant told Elijah that he saw "a little cloud like a man's hand is rising from the sea" (1 Kings 18:41–44). That little cloud was all the sign that Elijah needed to announce that the downpour was coming: "And in a little while the heavens grew black with clouds and wind, and there was a great rain" (1 Kings 18:45). Elijah could see at Mount Carmel how God's word could be trusted, on its own terms, and he knew how to take solace in the revelation of little things, foretelling great things. In the desert, he seems to have forgotten that, as do most of us. But this dynamic is consistent in the way God carries out his purposes. Seeming aloneness in the present is necessary for the future.

When pressed in by crowds of Greeks coming to see him, Jesus walked away, his attention turned toward the cross. This was no doubt inexplicable to many who followed him. After all, isn't this the ancient promise—that the nations would stream in to the kingdom of God? Yes, it was. And Jesus said, "Truly truly, I say to you, unless a grain of wheat falls into the earth and dies, it remains alone; but if it dies, it bears much fruit" (John 12:24). Looking to the cross—the moment of his most profound isolation and loneliness—Jesus said, "And I, when I am lifted up from the earth, will draw all people to myself" (John 12:32). The loneliness of Gethsemane and Golgotha was necessary for the community of Pentecost and the New Jerusalem. Whether for Jesus or for Paul, the language of "remnant" functioned in the same way, to demonstrate that integrity is not determined by popularity.

The rejection of the gospel by the crowds around Jesus, he said, was seen beforehand by the prophet Isaiah, who is told that the judgment of God would be seen in the blindness of people to his glory, glory Isaiah had seen in the temple and that John wrote was Jesus himself (Isa. 6:1–13; John 12:36–41). This rejection seems like failure, as did the refusal of most of the covenant community to respond to the apostles' preaching of the gospel. But such was always expected. The rejection would persist until, as Isaiah put it, the ground is desolate and burned over, until only the stump of a felled tree is left, and out of that stump would sprout a branch (Isa. 6:11–13). The seed that goes silently into the ground grows into a vine onto which the people of God, both the natural Israelite branches and the grafted-on branches from outside, find life and growth (Rom. 9–11).

The apostle Paul stood alone against both false teachers and dissembling disciples. When Simon Peter refused to eat with Gentiles while in Galatia, Paul saw this for what it was: not integrity but fear. "For before certain men came from James, he was eating with the Gentiles; but when they came he drew back and separated himself, fearing the circumcision party," Paul wrote. "And the rest of the Jews acted hypocritically along with him so that even Barnabas was led astray by their hypocrisy. But when I saw their conduct was not in step with the truth of the gospel, I said to Cephas before them all, 'If you, though a Jew, live like a Gentile and not like a Jew, how can you force the Gentiles to live like Jews?" (Gal. 2:12–14). Paul here was not a contrarian, separating himself out from the community. Instead, like Elijah, his dissent at this point was necessary in order to be consistent with the community of which he was heir. As he wrote elsewhere to the church at Rome, he was careful to explain that their definition of belonging would have excluded Abraham himself, who was judged right before God before he was circumcised (Rom. 4:1–25). Paul was not a pioneer but an heir.

Peter's case, and those with him, represented but a momentary instance of wobbling, one that could be corrected by the rebuke of a fellow apostle. The false teachers, on the other hand, Paul utterly repudiated, because they falsely taught that only those who conform to the covenant through the sign of circumcision were true heirs of God's promises in Christ. But in both cases, Paul opposed them not to distinguish himself from the community, nor to defend his honor or intelligence or fidelity against polemicists (something he refused to do elsewhere). Of the false teachers, Paul wrote "to them we did not yield in submission even for a moment, so that"—and this is the crucial point—"the truth of the gospel might be preserved for you" (Gal. 2:5). The false gospel seemed "normal" at that time and place. But Paul did not seem to care about being in the mainstream of his immediate context. He knew the Law and the Prophets, and the gospel he had received from Jesus.

Because Paul stood alone, we can stand together. That means countless numbers of us from every tribe, tongue, and nation; some of us on earth right now, and some of us in heaven. Like Elijah with Ahab and Baal, Paul could have had immediate "community" if he had simply embraced, or stayed silent about, what the gatekeepers insisted on to be part of that community. But, to do that, he would have sacrificed those with no voice, not just those without power in Galatia, but those of us who were millennia away from even being born.

This means you.

And the same is your calling, for the sake of others. You should seek counsel from those wiser than you, but you do not quit what God has called you to do just because you are criticized for it, or because people don't seem to pay much attention to it. You shouldn't quit teaching in that literacy project for the poor because people think it's a waste of time. You shouldn't stop your evangelism initiative with refugees just because people are afraid of them. You shouldn't silence Christian orthodoxy or Christian orthopraxy just because it hasn't been seen in a while in your mission field (or, harder still, in your church). Whatever it is that God has called you to do, recognize that if there weren't people who hate what you're doing, that would only be because you were not doing anything needed. You endure naysayers for the sake of those God has called you to serve (sometimes the future selves of those same naysayers!).

Giving oneself up for the community, in the long-term, often means loneliness in the short-term. Athanasius had to stand "against the world" in order to conserve the truth of the deity of Christ, when it seemed everyone was ready to deny it. Martin Luther had to step out from the monastery, alone, to question whether the selling of indulgences was consistent with the gospel of grace revealed in Scripture. Roger Williams had to walk, alone, into the wilderness of colonial America because the Puritan leaders of Massachusetts wouldn't brook dissent on questions of conscience. These figures served not in spite of their loneliness but through it.

Across the world, dissident movements against tyranny rise and fall, often without any notice from the rest of the population. But, even now over thirty years later, an image persists that has become almost an insignia of freedom-seekers everywhere, of a young, unknown Chinese man standing, alone, in Tiananmen Square against a row of tanks. What was striking at the moment, and is striking still, is that he was not part of a mob or a riot or an army. It was just him, unarmed and unaccompanied. And yet, that's where the power was. Part of the reason the world paid such attention is because this action didn't seem to make sense. Why would one person risk his life and his place in society without the means to fight back? And why would he do it without the safety of a herd? His courage, even in solitude, was empowered by what he trusted in, which was the power of his ideals—not in his place of belonging. The temptation in every generation is to do the reverse: to sacrifice the future by placating the present.

Often, we will speak of the church's need to "contextualize"—that is, to make our message understandable, if not palatable—to those around us, and that is a true part of the church's mission. But, if we are faithful to the gospel, we will contextualize not only to the present (whoever is in front of us right now), but also to the past (to our story of where God has met his people), and to the future (to those who are not yet Christians or may not yet even be born). In the face of that, we must stand by our words, and by our silences. The temptation of anyone in the middle of all of that is to despair of everything and to assume that the gospel is gone, that the future is irretrievable. But, in every age, there is a remnant, and, in every age, that remnant has a future.

Sometimes those outside the kingdom can see this principle better than those of us inside can. Leadership expert Seth Godin, for instance, writes about how what some call "the resistance"—that pressure inside not to do what we know we should do for fear of being criticized or ostracized—is self-defeating. Everything that disrupts any status quo will be criticized, and the pioneer threatened with exile. And nothing will be universally received and loved, unless it is, again, the status quo. But every development starts with people willing to risk that sort of censure, for the sake of others who are to come. He writes, "If you cater to the normal, you will disappoint the weird. And as the world gets weirder, that's a dumb strategy."[3] Actually it always was (1 Cor. 1:21–31; 4:1–20).

This hardly means that everything that is contrary to the status quo is right, by no means. Many times, the status quo is right and faithful, and those who seek to upend it are doing so in order to tear down what God has set up. The worshippers of Baal within Israel started out as a kind of "remnant" too, one that was later embraced by the whole community. And that's why Elijah devoted much effort to communicating that he was not, in fact, saying anything "new," but was instead calling his people back to, as Jude would put it later, "the faith that was once for all delivered to the saints" (Jude 3).

When Elijah confronted the prophets of Baal, he built the altar out of twelve stones. Why twelve? This was, the Scripture reveals, "according to the number of the tribes of the sons of Jacob, to whom the word of the LORD came, saying, 'Israel shall be your name'" (1 Kings 18:31). This echoes back to the entrance of the people across the Jordan into the land of promise. Joshua had told the people to mark out twelve men who would each carry a stone on his shoulder, "according to the number of the tribes of the people of Israel" (Josh. 4:5–6). This pile of stones was to be a reminder that the nation of Israel came not from native strength, but from promise, that they started not as a mighty nation but as twelve sons. Israel had started as a remnant. Often, refusing to conform to, as Paul put it, "the pattern of this world" around you (Rom. 12:2 NIV) is not just for your well-being. It allows you to serve others in the future, a community of people whose names you don't yet know, whose faces you cannot yet see, a people who may not yet be born the first time much less born again. Many times, it takes loneliness to get there.

And yet, like Elijah, courage eventually reveals that we are not, even at the point of our deepest loneliness, as alone as we think we are. Of course, Elijah was, in the wilderness, before the face of God, but God is often hidden from us. Elijah did not just have God with him (though that, of course, would be enough) but that 7,000 who, along with him, wouldn't bow the knee to the idols. The full ramifications of this would not be evident until the future, but they were, in some sense, a present reality. "I will leave for myself seven thousand in Israel," God said, with the clear implication being that at least some of them may well be there now. Elijah was not, in fact, alone. And, no matter what you are going through, neither are you.

One longtime observer of cultural movements and fads said to me that the primary challenge for the next generation of Christians is not a set of talking points on certain issues, but instead is the answer to one simple question: "Who do we mean, first, when we say 'we'?" If the answer is a generational cohort or a political faction or a nation-state or an ethnic group-ing, then we are rudderless. We are only able to find community in these little temporal groupings if we first see ourselves as the "we" of the body of Christ. But that community transcends the confines of space and time.

That's why the book of Hebrews says: "Therefore, since we are surrounded by so great a cloud of witnesses, let us also lay aside every weight, and sin which clings so closely, and let us run with endurance the race that is set before us, looking to Jesus, the founder and perfecter of our faith, who for the joy that was set before him endured the cross, despising the shame, and is seated at the right hand of the throne of God" (Heb. 12:1–2). It is not just that we have a community behind us, in the past, of people to whom God was faithful, but rather that this communion is a present reality, though one we cannot see. And that community includes solitary old Elijah. Without even naming individual names, the writer of Hebrews spoke of those "of whom the world was not worthy," who spent their lives "wandering about in deserts and mountains, and in dens and caves of the earth" (Heb. 11:38). After passing through a time of loneliness, we find that God often fits us together with a community of people who also have walked through loneliness, and we will see that, often, this is a community we would not have chosen on our own.

God did this with Elijah, by speaking to him of Elisha, who was to become a son to him in the faith. But, really, Elijah had seen God work this way before. After he had announced God's initial judgment on Ahab, God sent him on the run eastward toward the Jordan, and then off into Zarephath, where he met a widow. Most of the time we focus on the fact that Elijah helped this woman, and he did—providing oil in her jug miraculously, and then raising her son from the dead (1 Kings 17:8–24), but we sometimes fail to see that the widow also rescued Elijah, feeding him, housing him, and relieving his solitude (1 Kings 17:15).

Ironically, this was the home region of Baal and the foreign gods. While in the land of God, Elijah saw Baal; while in the land of Baal, Elijah saw God. God formed a community quite different from the one expected, a community that was, like Elijah would be, not at the center but on the margins. This is the dynamic to which Jesus pointed in his inaugural sermon in the synagogue in Nazareth. That's where Jesus said, "No prophet is acceptable in his hometown" (Luke 4:24), a statement much misunderstood over the years. Some have interpreted this as meaning that someone can't really minister to people who changed his or her diapers as a baby, since they won't respect that person. That may or may not be true, but it has nothing to do with what Jesus was saying. Jesus, instead, was confronting exactly what Elijah confronted—the idea of a folk religion in which the religion is a tool to maintain the interests of the present community itself. The context was the demand that Jesus do the signs and wonders for his hometown crowd that he had done elsewhere, almost as "constituent service." Jesus, though, isolated himself by clarifying that the community God forms does not necessarily conform to the natural lines of blood and soil. "But in truth, I tell you, there were many widows in Israel in the days of Elijah, when the heavens were shut up three years and six months and a great famine came over all the land," Jesus taught, "and Elijah was sent to none of them but only to Zarephath, in the land of Sidon, to a woman who was a widow" (Luke 4:25–26).

And, of course, that's what Jesus does, not only with Elijah, but all the time. He formed a community during his initial earthly ministry that was incoherent—made up of those who had been fishermen from Galilee, tax collectors in collaboration with Rome, zealots who had been in resistance against Rome, religious leaders who had studied the Law, prostitutes who had been cast out of the community. Then after his resurrection, he formed a church made up of Jews and Gentiles, fused into one new humanity, and organically part of the same body, with all parts needing the others. That dynamic was at work when Jesus called out a would-be serial killer on his way to execute the church in Syria, and then made him apostle to the nations. And the first thing Jesus did was to see to it that the new convert was cared for by a Syrian Christian. This was not welcome by either of these two parties, for obvious reasons. But Jesus formed an unlikely community, a community that could only be forged on the loneliness of the margins. And that community pointed toward the further disruptions that would come, that would necessitate a lonely Paul standing by himself for the sake of a community yet to be born.

In order for that to happen, there must be an exile first, a pulling apart from the "normal" bonds of community, so that one, perhaps even in desperation, can find the community one cannot imagine that one needs. Think back to the loneliest times in your own life, to the people God sent to you. They are probably not the people you would have chosen for yourself.

This happens because the communities on which we depend are often merely natural—formed by bonds of family or accidents of geography or commonality of interest or circumstance.

The gospel does not eradicate these, by any means. Jesus cared for his mother, and arranged for her care after his departure, all the way to the end of her life, and commands us to do the same. But when this is the only form of community, it can easily devolve into what we often see around us—utilitarian "communities" where each person exists because of what he or she can "do" for us. This does not pull us toward love.

In order to learn to love in a Christlike, self-sacrificial way—even toward those we would "naturally" love even if God did not exist—we must learn to love those we don't "need," those we would not otherwise even see, maybe even those we've been taught to hate. That's especially true in a time when, as C. S. Lewis once put it, "caucus has replaced friendship."[4] What he meant by that is that we tend to, consciously or unconsciously, form relationships with people in exactly this kind of utilitarian manner—where we determine their value mostly by what they can do for us. Maybe you've experienced that, where you start to realize that someone's kindness to you turned out to really be about making a romantic connection with a friend of yours, or getting a promotion at work, or to get votes in a political campaign, or any other such means to an end. You likely, at some point, said something along the lines of, "I feel so used." And we all have had the feeling at some point that we are being manipulated, that someone is using the resources of human connection to get something from us.

The only time I ever really saw my mother angry was, when we were small children, a photographer taking pictures of my brothers and me tried to get her to purchase the most expensive packet of photographs. When my mother demurred, the sales person said, "I really hope that one of these precious children is not run over by a car and killed, because you will wish you had every photograph you could have of them."

My mother calmly, but memorably, rebuked her, and then grabbed our hands as we walked out. She, rightly, recognized that this person was cynically using the fear of grief and loss for crass commercial benefit; she was using something of weight and sacredness for her own ends. Most people aren't that ham-handed in their manipulation, but all of us have experienced a sense of being treated this way. And then this leads us to ask where else we are being used, that we just can't see?

Sometimes a new, or renewed, vision is exactly what is required. As Wendell Berry wrote, "If change is to come, then, it will have to come from the outside. It will have to come from the margins." After all, Berry notes, "It was the desert, not the temple, that gave us the prophets; the colonies, not the motherland, that gave us Adams and Jefferson." Berry argues that this sort of marginalization is necessary to get insight on what really matters, apart from the urgencies of livelihood and status in the community. "The encrusted religious structure is not changed by its institutional dependents—they are part of the crust," he writes. "It is changed by one who goes alone to the wilderness, where he fasts and prays and returns with cleansed vision." The one who goes to the margins, though, is not to be one who is a contrarian or a curmudgeon, let alone one who rages against right revelation and authority. As Berry concludes, "He returns to the community, not necessarily with new truth, but with a new vision of the truth; he sees it more whole than before."[5] The story of Scripture and the history since bears out this pattern.

Biblical community, in fact, is not about power or status but about something else entirely. After Paul's Elijah-like wanderings in Arabia, he told the Galatian church that he had been to Jerusalem, where he had met Jesus' brother James and other important figures in the Jerusalem church. This was, though, not in any way the basis of his authority, hence he waited three years in Arabia and back to Damascus before he ever went. And then, years later, he went to Jerusalem again, to meet with these prominent leaders. "And from those who seemed to be influential (what they were makes no difference to me; God shows no partiality)—those, I say, who seemed influential added nothing to me" (Gal. 2:6). Paul here makes clear that he and these apostles were part of the same mission, and received one another as such, but he in no way sought to hide himself under the influence of their fame or impressiveness or influence. And he wrote, when he left to carry out his mission to the nations with their blessing: "Only, they asked us to remember the poor, the very thing I was eager to do" (Gal. 2:10).

Why was this—the poor—of such importance to Paul and to the other apostles? It's because they operated under a long-term view of influence and of community—and by "long term" I mean trillions and trillions of years. The poor aren't simply lacking in resources, but are on the margins of any given community because they don't have the leverage to do anything for anyone. The Proverbs say, "Whoever is generous to the poor lends to the LORD, and he will repay him for his deed" (Prov. 19:17). The poor are not able to contribute to the carnal aspects of power—around which so much "community," it turns out, hinges.

No one cannot bask in the overflow of the glory of the poor and the marginalized, because they have none. Instead, to find community there, you must recognize what James wrote, "Listen, my beloved brothers, has God not chosen those who are poor in the world to be rich in faith, and heirs of the kingdom?" (James 2:5). When we find community with the divorced single mother who doesn't know from where her next rent payment will come, or the recovering heroin addict who is just this side of a relapse, or the refugee family struggling to learn the language and to fend off insults from those who see their very presence as a threat, or the cognitively disabled young woman whose mother wishes she had aborted her, we start to recognize how the kingdom of God arrives. And when we not only serve such people—as Elijah did to the widow of Zarephath—but are served by the gifts God has given such people (as the widow served Elijah), we start to see that our place in God's kingdom is not based, as it is in so many fallen-human communities, in the transactional, but on something else—on the love of the Father, on the blood of the Son, on the unity of the Spirit. Often to get us there, God must dissolve those transactional and self-serving communities of protection in order to get us to authentic love. That's the way gospel community often comes together, through the crucible of loneliness. That's terrifying but necessary.

In Christianity, this is especially important because, such disruptions of the status quo, calling the community back to a "first love" (Rev. 2:4), are what keep the church grounded in the transcendent Scriptures rather than in natural forms of belonging and adjusting.

That's why one sociologist warned, in the middle of the so-called "Christian century" that "Christian America" had created a religion in which the religion was valued for helping people to "adjust." Christian America taught people to be "at home in the society and the universe," and, as such, rendered "incomprehensible" the "zeal" of an Elijah, an Amos, or a Jesus. That's because the very purpose of this nominal form of religion was to "protect him against such perils," that is the perils of loneliness and isolation and "strangeness," and, indeed, it "protects him so well that it makes the prophetic faith of the Bible almost unintelligible to him."[6] Whenever that happens, God will provide a voice to say "You"—the person who will stand alone at judgment, who cannot hide in a crowd—"You must be born again." When we find ourselves at home in the cosmos, God will remind us—usually via a voice from the wilderness—that we have here no abiding homeland, but are seeking a different city (Heb. 11:13–16).

In fact, studies demonstrate that a key factor in a person's inability to accurately perceive reality has to do with the way certain individuals, of all types, absorb themselves into networks of people who are just like them, what some scholars call "homophily."[7] It turns out that "birds of a feather flock together" reasoning leads us to the place where we don't accurately read ourselves or the world around us. Perhaps this is one reason God created human beings to live in communities in which there is both similarity and difference. "It is not good for the man to be alone," God said in the beginning (Gen. 2:18 NIV). The answer to that was not for God to create a clone-like reflection of Adam, but instead one who is both "bone of his bone and flesh of his flesh," but differing. In the same way, the church that Jesus put together includes the similarities of common human experience, of both created dignity and sinful need, but the differences of male/female, Jew/Greek, and so on, are all within the mysterious unity of the same body (Gal. 3:28–29).

At the end of it all, though, is God's purpose of joining, in our own lives, the personal and the communal. In God's purpose, the personal is necessary for true community—we cannot be a mass of bees in a hive and genuinely know love. In God's purpose, likewise, the community is necessary for the personal. We cannot be who we really are without the experience of loving and being loved, serving and being served. In some sense, one does not even need revelation to see this. Psychologists will speak of the need for adolescents to find "individuation," that is to discover which of their values and principles is really theirs, and what is just the mimicking of their parents' unquestioned assumptions. That's why parents shouldn't panic when their children, at a certain age, start to seem unmoored. This can be tumultuous at the moment, but that sort of discovery is much better then than in the middle of life. Others will speak of the necessity of maturity found in, as one puts it, "differentiation within a relationship, not independence of it."[8] What this means is a combination of separateness and closeness, in which the person avoids both "cutoff"—the splintering away into one's silo—and "fusion"—the absorption of the person's thoughts, feelings, identity, and maybe even conscience into some group. While anyone can observe this need, the gospel—reaching all the way back to lonely Elijah in the wilderness and beyond—shows us why this is the case.

In Christ, God has joined together the personal and the communal. In the gospel, we see that we cannot hide in our tribe or bloodline or ethnicity or family or religion, but we must come into the family of God one-by-one, through the newness of new birth (John 3:3). We are not birthed into a vacuum but into a kingdom, into a family. Like a body the church functions together, serving one another and worshipping the same Lord (1 Cor. 12:12–31). And yet, for the sake of community past and community future, sometimes lonely voices must speak alone, calling the people away from the herd and toward the narrow way. The fact that the most "Christianized" places in this country are also among the loneliest should be alarming to us; a picture of just how far we have drifted from the biblical picture of the gospel, which balances the personal and the communal, the one and the many, the individual and the community. In Christ alone, we are in Christ, together. And in Christ together, we are in Christ, alone.

I was wrong about "Me and Jesus." But, in some ways, maybe so was the man who wrote it. As much as he said he didn't need the church, that he could go it alone, he actually couldn't even sing the song that way. Tom T. Hall wrote that as a child he didn't go to church, but that he grew up standing on his porch on Sunday mornings listening to the Mount Pisgah

United Methodist Church, an African-American congregation a half mile from his home, singing their hymns. That's where he turned when a collaborator warned him that "'Me and Jesus' would require a lot of backup voices."[9]

And so in that recording studio, the white and black singers sang together, something that never would have been allowed by the cultural community norms of the Kentucky of Hall's childhood. Those community norms would have kept them apart; "Me and Jesus" could bring them together. That alone, of course, would do hardly anything about segregation and racial injustice; many, many more "backup voices" would be needed for that. But the suffering and the isolation, much of it brought about by stifling, conformity-enforcing community, was something the homeless people in my little ad-hoc flock could understand, even when their preacher could not.

Finding courage will sometimes mean finding the courage to stand alone, to stand with communities one would never have chosen for oneself. And courage will also mean that genuine community comes often through deep loneliness—often solitude in the short-run is the means to belonging. That's why we will often encounter Jesus the most intensely when we feel the most alone, but we will learn there that he has been with us all along, and is leading us toward others who have been lonely too. We need to know how to sing with a number that no man can number, with a church that is stretched out across the millennia, bridging heaven and earth. But along the way we will learn that, between here and there, are moments of profound loneliness, when we learn that our only ultimate audience is the one before Whom we will stand in the end.

When we pay attention, we will hear a lot of backup singers in the background of the music of our lives, and we will find ourselves singing backup in the music of countless other lives. We will find that we must learn how to sing "Me and Jesus," but we will find that we cannot sing it alone.

# Chapter Seven

# Courage and Justice

## *Righteousness through Irrelevance*

Several years ago, a friend of mine was consulted by a white evangelical church in Birmingham as to why their church was in such precipitous decline, given their storied history of success. At the time of the white supremacist bombing of the 16th Street Baptist Church across town, a terrorist attack that killed four young girls, the white church had pews packed with people and budgets flush with cash. On the morning of those murders, the white church was probably silent. Many of the worshippers in the white church probably reflected the viewpoints of those around them, that the struggle for civil rights was a "political" problem, being driven by "outside agitation"

and probably inspired by "Marxists." While civil rights pro-
testers were beaten and assaulted with fire hoses in the streets,
while Sunday-school children saw the stained-glass face of Jesus
blown apart, only seconds before they saw his real face looking
back at them in eternity, the white church no doubt concluded
that they would avoid "politics" and "social justice" concerns.
That was what the liberals did. They would just stick to "simple
gospel preaching."

Left unsaid was the fact that the members of that church had
no objection to all sorts of other "political" pronouncements, on
prayer-in-schools Supreme Court decisions, for instance. But
anything more than vague abstractions on something the Bible
speaks to unambiguously and repeatedly—the "one blood"
humanity in the image of God, the necessity of reconciliation in
the body of Christ, justice for those who are oppressed—would
have created a firestorm in the congregation. Controversy would
have ensued—maybe even resulting in the near-unanimous
firing of the pastor and maybe the social isolation of the dea-
cons—if the church had dared to open membership to their
fellow Christians who were black, or if they sought to baptize
African-American people who came to faith in Christ.

As the years marched on, the area became majority black.
The congregation dwindled to a small band of elderly whites
who now lived in the suburbs and drove in on Sundays. They
tried, they said, to "reach out" to the church's African-American

neighbors, but they couldn't get them to join. What they couldn't see is that the church had already sent their message to those neighbors—back when the church didn't need those neighbors to survive.

What was behind the reluctance to do the right thing? For many churches, no doubt it was a moral blindness, an accommodation to the world around them such that they could not see what was wrong with what they were doing. For others, it was a willful choice, to obey the dictates of Jim Crow rather than Jesus Christ, knowing in their hearts that they were disobeying the will of their Lord. But there were no doubt others whose consciences knew that the pattern around them was wrong. For many of them, a driver behind this behavior was a fear of losing relevance.

After all, a leader who went against the "southern way of life" would have lost his or her ministry place immediately. And laypeople who did so would be deemed "odd" at best or "liberal" and subversive at worst. Some probably believed something would have to be done, eventually, against these injustices, but that they would have to conserve their relevance in order to do so. "If I'm gone," they might have thought, "they will just replace me with someone self-consciously racist, who will never get the church where it needs to be." They would have sought to protect their "relevance" to the people, as they were, in the pews. Maybe the church itself understood that this kind of segregation was wrong, but they might have concluded that, were they to accept black members, they would lose the ability to reach the white people in their area, the majority, who mostly would have been "uncomfortable" in an integrated church, for fear that their children might fall in love one day with a non-white peer and want to marry. Moreover, the church probably thought that speaking about these issues would "go over the heads" of their people, who wouldn't see the relevance of such concerns to their lives. The irony is that this church not only did away with its moral integrity by their actions, but they also did away with the very thing they sought to preserve, their relevance, in the long run. Their complicity with injustice not only brought them on the wrong side of Jesus, but also sacrificed their future in order to placate the present.

And behind that was a skewed vision of who is really "important" and "significant." In the book of Revelation, the "Beast" of power and influence and the false prophets praising it seem to be influential. But those who sit on the only thrones that survive the apocalypse to come are beheaded martyrs, the last people with whom one would want to be seen or associated, for fear of losing one's own head too. And yet, they were the ones reigning with Christ (Rev. 20:4). And still are.

Now, it is far too easy to look back on the way previous generations accommodated themselves to injustices. That was, of course, Jesus' warning to the religious leaders of his time:

"For you build the tombs of the prophets and decorate the monuments of the righteous, saying, 'If we had lived in the days of our fathers, we would not have taken part with them in shedding the blood of the prophets'" (Matt. 23:29–30). But the truth is that this phenomenon, of shrinking back in the face of injustice, is not isolated to any previous generation, but is always happening, in every time. And this sort of accommodation is not just the case in epoch-defining issues of social injustice, as with the regime of Jim Crow, but often happens in the quieter, more ordinary decisions of everyday life.

Sometimes the difficulty comes with not knowing what the right thing to do is. There are often circumstances when that becomes a real dilemma. The Christian who works in military intelligence grapples with whether or not it is lying to take on an undercover identity as someone who is of another religion, for instance, and will have to "worship" along with others. Consider the couple who come to the conviction that human life begins at conception, but then do not know what to do with the embryos they fertilized, now kept in freezers, when they were undergoing fertility treatments years before. Or consider the woman who wonders if her husband's several-times-now infidelities, after which he always claims to be repentant, constitutes biblical grounds for divorce. There are always going to be moments where we want to do the right thing, if only we could discern what it is.

The bigger challenge, though, for a life of courage is not such situations, but the more typical one, in which we know, deep in our consciences, what the right thing to do is, but we lack the bravery to do it. Sometimes—as we have seen before—that timidity comes from a fear of someone else's power or of losing our place in the community, but often it is not just these things but also the sense that the way of injustice is seemingly permanent. The seeming permanence causes many to conclude that these unjust practices or structures are "just the way the world is," and that taking a "realistic" view means simply accepting such things. We start, then, to conclude that whatever is unjust is just normal. Or we start to despair of any ability for any of these things to change.

Along with that, then, comes the tendency to seek to conserve one's "relevance" to "the real world." In such cases, our reading of the "way things are, and always will be" empowers not courage but cowardice. And often that has to do with what group we see as mattering to our own status, and what group is expendable in order to get or to maintain that status. Think of, for instance, the high school student who sees the bullied, lonely student by herself at the cafeteria table, but is scared to sit with her, for fear that this will mean that he, too, will be excluded from his friends, and will join her in her loneliness. That tendency, sadly, does not go away with graduation, but is the persistent pull all of life.

Even in nursing homes, this same dynamic is at work: "Really? You're sitting with Gladys? You like her?" And so, what most people do is simply accommodate themselves to the "way things are," conforming not just their actions but, in time, their consciences to "reality" in such a way that, after a while, they don't even wrestle with the morality of their choices anymore at all. And some people work against the injustice to the point of exhaustion—wondering when they look around and see injustice persisting whether their efforts were all a waste of time and effort. Some accommodate to the injustice, and some are exhausted by it.

When we see and recognize ongoing injustice—that seems not to have any resolution in sight—we are often troubled, wondering if any of the institutions or relationships or moral norms on which we relied to keep us safe can be trusted anymore. The word people often use to describe such a feeling is "shaken." After a man with overwhelming evidence of having committed murder was acquitted by a jury, one of the victim's family members spoke of how this "shook" her "faith in the system." I've heard similar statements from people after seeing a person found guilty of a crime and imprisoned for years only later to have been proven innocent. If these acts of injustice can happen in the systems we trust to protect us, the reasoning goes, who then is really safe? This sort of crisis can happen anywhere—in a family, in a neighborhood, in a government, in a church, in a workplace.

This reality is in the backdrop of the Elijah encounter with God on the mountain. His complaint was not just about his dangerous personal future, but also a question of justice, namely in terms of his frustrated zeal. After the point of silence on the mountain, God reiterated again his question from before: "What are you doing here, Elijah?" And Elijah said, once again, "I have been very jealous for the LORD, the God of hosts. For the people of Israel have forsaken your covenant, thrown down your altars, and killed your prophets with the sword, and I, even I only, am left, and they seek my life, to take it away" (1 Kings 19:14). That language of "jealous" is related to the idea, prominent in both the Old and New Testaments, of "zeal." Both words are potentially misunderstood in our context.

We tend to think of "zeal" in terms of enthusiasm or excitement: "She is really full of zeal about this new corporate branding initiative," or "No one can match his zeal for the Los Angeles Lakers." Likewise, "jealous" in our day tends to be thought of only in terms of possessiveness in a relationship or even envy of other people. "He's so jealous that he keeps checking on his girlfriend's whereabouts to make sure she's not with some other guy," or "She's just jealous because she's not the one who won the promotion."

Both words in Elijah's context connote not just enthusiasm but a specific sort of driven motivation toward justice—toward the ordering of things aright. Elijah's zeal had not led to such righteousness, but instead here he was: wasting away again at the margins of the nation. Elijah's failure was not, in his view, just about his own life, but about the failure of justice.

God's response, though, was not a reassurance of Elijah's significance through a "This Is Your Life" sort of panorama of why he was more successful than he knows. Instead, God directed Elijah away from himself altogether, toward a mission to seek out and anoint three others—Hazael as king of Aram, Jehu as king of Israel, and Elisha as prophet in Elijah's place—through whom God would bring about justice. The house of Ahab appeared to evade justice, but they were headed for a reckoning. And, in this enigmatic response, God revealed something about the "what," the "who," and the "how" of justice—questions that are with us, and if not on the surface then just under it in your life right now.

The "what" of justice was, first of all, a reminder that God is indeed a God of justice, that this matters to him. Elijah seems to have concluded that there is nothing else that can be done. The nation has gone along with the king's direction, and all that is left for Elijah to do—as the last one standing—is to go away into death. But God foretold another scenario—one that the rest of the books of the Kings would show playing out. Hazael would indeed come in terror against disobedient Israel. And Jehu would be the one who would wipe out not only Jezebel, but would also completely dismantle the dynasty of Ahab and turn the altars of Baal into a toilet (2 Kings 9:30–10:27).

These two kings were hardly heroes in this story. Hazael comes to office as a result of smothering a sick man to death with a washcloth. Jehu ended up following in some of the same old idolatrous ways as his forefathers. Some have suggested that God working through immoral people in this way is a signal that Christians should embrace immoral means to get to a just end, something God elsewhere expressly forbids (Rom. 12:21). God is sovereign over life and death, means and ends, in a way that no human being is, and God is choosing these figures to carry out judgment against his own covenant people, in the same way he would later use the Assyrians, the Babylonians, and the Romans. Indeed, God even turns the Devil's actions (intended by him to be evil) against him, and toward the purposes of God's grace and glory. That is certainly no sign that Christians should pray to the Devil (God, literally, forbid) in order to carry out good ends. The point was that God would, ultimately, see to it that the seemingly permanent House of Ahab would fall. This is important for Elijah to know, right at this point, to keep him from ultimately tipping over into despairing resignation or, who knows, maybe even into a kind of disgruntled accommodation with the "way things are."

This is important because the drivers of any injustice or immorality always do so by pretending to be inevitable and permanent. The consequences for joining in such things, because they are not immediately perceptible, are thought to be absent altogether. In the first book of the Bible, the serpent of Eden, therefore, can say to Eve, "You will not surely die" if you transgress God's command (Gen. 3:4). And in the last book of the Bible, the crowds (including the office of "prophet") say: "Who is like the beast, and who can fight against it?" (Rev. 13:4). This sense of apparent powerlessness is weaponized into approving of or joining in with what the conscience knows to be immoral or unjust. That need not happen in some cosmic-seeming event that one would think seems to come right out of the biblical apocalypse. It happens every day when, for instance, an employee seethes internally but does nothing about the fact that he knows his supervisor is embezzling money from the firm or erupting into verbally abusive tirades against subordinates or sexually harassing the woman who works with him. The implicit message is, "This is the way it is here, and always will be. If you want to keep your status, or get ahead, you are just going to have to get on board with this."

The first step toward justice, though, is the unveiling that the powers of such injustice are not as permanent as they pretend. The illusion of inevitability and invincibility is then broken. Jesus spoke of a wealthy man who stored up his goods in barns, and, satisfied, said to himself: "Soul, you have ample goods laid up for many years; relax, eat, drink, be merry," to which God replied, "Fool! This night your soul is required of you, and the things you have prepared, whose will they be?" (Luke 12:19–20). The man believed that his present reality would always be the case, and was then crushed by its ultimate impermanence. This was the message God sent to rulers from Pharaoh to Nebuchadnezzar to Belshazzar. Even among those who are biblically illiterate, the sayings drawn from some of these accounts are still used: "feet of clay," or "The handwriting is on the wall," or "weighed in the balance and found wanting." That extends to the picture of Babylon the Great that seemed so wealthy and permanent and yet in the span of one hour was to be rubble in the sea (Rev. 18:10).

This is not just a warning to those powers that exalt themselves, but also an encouragement to those who suffer under them. In the bloodthirsty "Cultural Revolution" led by the Chinese Communist Party, the brutal suppression of religion there was meant to dismantle any possible point of alternative loyalty to the dictator Mao Zedong. Mao took on the role of a kind of deity in a cult of personality. But, as one observer notes, "There was one problem with Mao as a living god: he died."[1] This death did not, of course, free the country from tyranny, but it was a reminder—both to those who had merged themselves with Maoism and those who dissented from it—that no human being, and no human empire, is permanent. This was the message of God to Elijah: he had a plan for the world of Ahab and Jezebel to come to an end, and, by including Elisha in the list of coming figures God emphasized that this end would be the end result of the Word of God. The injustices of the powers-that-be seemed unchangeable, with no one left who could even dissent from them, but, as one preacher in my tradition put it years ago, there would be "payday someday."

God did not reveal, so far as we know, in this encounter what would be the presenting event leading to this righting of wrongs. But we see in the text later that the wheel of justice was set in motion by an obnoxious act of injustice on the part of Ahab and Jezebel. The precipitating event was Elijah's confrontation with Ahab over the vineyard of a peasant. In that encounter, Ahab was provoked, once again, by a kind of narcissistic injury, embarrassed by a prophet, and "vexed and sullen," he slinked back to Samaria. There Ahab became enamored with the vineyard of a man named Naboth, and asked for it to be sold to him, so the king could refit it into a vegetable garden. Naboth's response—"The LORD forbid that I should give you the inheritance of my fathers"—provoked another round of sulking from Ahab (1 Kings 21:1–4). Jezebel, though, vowed, just as she had to kill Elijah, to get the vineyard for her groom. This was rooted in a sense of entitlement. "Do you now govern Israel?" she asked, as though that office would mean that he could run roughshod over the property of his subjects. Jezebel then used the power of both "church" and "state" to act unjustly toward Naboth. She called a fast day—a religious rite meant to worship God—in order to set up Naboth. She had false witnesses testify against him. And then she sought the execution of this peasant—again using the powers of the office of king of Israel—to satisfy her husband's appetites.

Here's why this matters in your life right now. It is not likely that you occupy the power of monarch, to put people to death at whim. In reality, even most kings and queens in our contemporary world lack such power. And yet, one could argue that in our time almost everybody can easily wield power that could rival that of Ahab and Jezebel. An air-traffic controller, arguably, has much more power over life and death than did an ancient Near Eastern king. And, if you are the citizen of a majority world democratic republic, you bear the ultimate accountability for weapons systems that could not just unhitch a farmer from his vineyard but could vaporize his entire region. And, of course, with modern communications technology, even the most powerless has the ability to spread falsehoods about someone else in ways that Jezebel, had she seen it, would have believed to be witchcraft. All of us are held accountable for the ways that we use power—whether in ways that are just and moral, or exploitative and sinful.

The problem with the fallen human conscience is that, while all of us recognize that there are standards of justice, we seek to protect our guilty consciences from thinking about how such standards keep us from doing the sins we want to commit. That is seen, for instance, usually in what we recognize as relevant to the discussion at all. Some people, for instance, chafe at biblical passages on personal morality as related to our sexual behavior. When the pastor preaches against adultery, the adulterer who does not wish to repent will often accuse the preacher of meddling in areas he does not understand. "Why would you be so obsessed with what two consenting adults do in their own bedrooms," he might say, "when there are poor children starving in our community and around the world?" And, at the same time, those who wish to keep a status quo of public injustice will often say that concerns in the realm of systems or courts are a "social justice distraction" from "simple gospel preaching."

Both those who wish to evade God's justice in areas of personal morality and those who wish to evade God's justice in areas of social relationships use similar tactics. The personally immoral person would say that focusing on such matters is "legalism," and is therefore a distraction from "God's grace." And the person who wishes to evade God's justice in the public or social realms will say that such talk is "political" or "social gospel" and therefore a distraction from the mission of the church. Is this sometimes the case, on both counts? Yes. Legalism is real. The person who says that she is right with God due to her sexual purity needs rebuke—such works can never accomplish God's favor. The reverse is not therefore true—"You are saved by grace, not by your sexual morality, so enjoy your orgy."

Can someone preach a gospel-free moralism that presents the Christian life as a matter of more effort in living out rules and regulations? Yes. And the Bible condemns such.

Does that mean that one should shun biblical direction on what morality is—what pleases God? If so, then the Bible is itself a "moralistic" book, devoting much effort to defining what life in Christ should look like in the way we live our lives as children, parents, husbands and wives, citizens, neighbors, employers and employees, and so on. The difference between "moralism" and "morality" is the difference between whether the morality is motivated and defined by the gospel, or whether the morality *is* the gospel.

Is there such a thing as a "social gospel" that rejects the gospel of Jesus Christ? Yes. Such a viewpoint rejects the necessity of the new birth, suggesting that the amelioration of social injustices can usher in the kingdom of God. Rejecting this does not mean that "social" questions are therefore outside of the scrutiny of God's revealed word anymore than a rejection of the possibility of sinless perfection in the personal arena means that the pursuit of holiness as defined by the Bible is "a drift toward works-righteousness."

Another tactic held in common is to say that any concern for personal morality is "Puritan" or "fundamentalist." And, the reverse side of the coin says that concern for justice in social matters is coming from unorthodox liberals or "Marxists" or "radicals" (this strategy was especially well-utilized by "Christian" defenses of human slavery, lynching, and Jim Crow segregation). Pharaoh loved his children (which is why he wailed at Passover). That is no reason to say that the command to love one's children is "Egyptian."

In reality, though, very few people in either aspect of this sort of endeavor actually believe what they are saying. Those who would imply that personal morality is a distraction from the gospel nonetheless actually believe the opposite. The person who would say that removing a pastor for adultery is wrong because "We are all broken, and God uses sinners" would almost always take a different view if the pastor were inviting church members to join his harem of concubines. And the person who would say that the Bible speaks to personal morality but not to "social justice" almost always speaks out against structural injustices when they happen to line up with his or her tribal commitments.

Is child pornography an issue of personal morality or social injustice? Both. The person who exploits children this way is personally sinning against God, and the groups of people who profit from or allow this to happen are guilty of a grave injustice as well. A jury, knowing a person is guilty of child pornography, that nonetheless exempts him from the law, cannot plead before God that their actions were not "immoral" because they acted in a public capacity, any more than Joseph's brothers or Pontius Pilate's court system can claim that because they were acting as a tribe or as a state that the "social justice" questions of selling a brother into slavery or crucifying an innocent man are irrelevant concerns. In fact, all the various ways of dividing up ethics into "private" or "social" in a way that exempts one or the other from moral scrutiny are not about arguing issues, but about protecting guilty consciences. We want to prop up our immorality, done on our own or in groups, done personally or by "giving approval to those who do such things" (Rom. 1:32), or we are afraid of those who do.

In our day and context, those who downplay the demands of Scripture on personal morality are trying to say "nobody can say anything about the way I choose to orgasm." And those who reject as "subversive" appeals for justice in the social arena are usually trying to say, "It's nobody's business how I treat black or brown people." Neither approach withstands the scrutiny of Scripture. Ahab and Jezebel face the judgment of God for their personal idolatry, for their leading the people of God, as religious officials, into such idolatry, and for using the levers of the courts and the military forces at their disposal to treat people in unjust ways. They sin against God *and* against neighbor. They sin as those with unclean lips *and* as a people of unclean lips. They sin alone and sin together; they sin as a couple and as a nation. A fornicator's morality and a slaveholder's ethic lead to the same place, apart from repentance and faith: to hell.

Years ago, I heard a pastor I knew to be supportive of abortion rights preach to a group of Christians I knew to be staunchly pro-life on abortion. When he came to the topic, he said, "If we would just teach our teenagers and young adults sexual chastity, we wouldn't have all these debates about abortion." The congregation said "Amen," not at all realizing what he was saying. He was saying that abortion should be dealt with as a personal issue of morality, but not as a matter of public justice. Many issues are, of course, that way. I believe envy is sinful, but not that it should be illegal. That's not the case, though, with the question of whether dependent, vulnerable human beings should be unprotected by law.

Is abortion a personal moral issue? Yes. Is abortion an issue of legal injustice—in which some persons are denied a right to life based upon their age and stage of dependency? Yes. Is abortion a matter of structural injustice—in which a predatory industry preys on desperate and vulnerable women? Yes. It is all of those things. The person who says, "I think unborn children are persons, but, as a citizen, I approve of depriving them of their rights because I don't think the gospel speaks to 'social justice' issues" is in serious error. So is the person who says, "I think abortion is unjust and ought to be illegal, but while it is legal, I am going to have one; don't blame me—blame the system."

Does the Bible give a comprehensive framework for what's right and wrong in the structuring of societies in carrying out justice? No. The Bible also doesn't give a comprehensive framework for what it means to be a moral individual or to be a moral family, if by that we mean a scenario-by-scenario detail of "do this and don't do that." In those areas that we deem "personal," some matters are explicit. Someone who says, "Pray for me this weekend that we get a good price for my niece that we are trying to traffic to a drug cartel" must be rebuked and brought to accountability immediately. Other matters, though, are spoken of at the level of principle but not at the level of specifics.

The Bible mandates that husbands and wives, for instance, should not withhold sexual relations from one another, except for short periods of time (1 Cor. 7:1–5), but a church that published calendars for "sex" and "no sex" days of the week just as they do daily Bible readings would be an authoritarian and wrongheaded church. And then on some issues, the Bible leaves questions of morality to individual consciences—whether for example to eat meat or only vegetables or whether to observe certain ceremonial days. In such cases, people should coexist and not attempt to force anyone else to act against conscience (Rom. 14:1–23).

The same is true on matters that we often try to divide out into "justice" issues. The Bible nowhere reveals what a tax rate should be, and anyone who says so is overstepping boundaries of authority. At the same time, someone who calls on people to stop paying taxes because "who is the government to ask this of us?" is in violation of Scripture (Matt. 22:17–22; Rom. 13:7). As with the so-called "personal" moral issues, some of these questions are left to prudence and judgment. Some of them are informed by principles, such as "love neighbor as self" although the specific applications may be debated. And others are explicit—do not defraud widows of their property; do not prosecute the innocent or exonerate the guilty in a court of law; and so on.

One might assume that the condemnation of injustice by Ahab and Jezebel is not relevant to one's own life. You are probably not a dictator of some government somewhere. And yet, the issue is not whether or not you have power that could harm others, but what degree of such power you have. Whatever that level is means accountability. Jesus never held the Galilean crowds accountable for Roman tax extortion. They had no power to change such things. But the tax collectors them-selves—Zacchaeus, for instance—were told to repent and make restitution. The man born blind received no instruction on whether to show mercy to the man beaten on the Jericho Road. He had no power to do so, and thus no responsibility. That was a different story for the priest and the Levite who saw the beaten man and stepped aside.

Perhaps you are an hourly worker in a grocery store. You have no accountability for your manager's spending habits and thus no responsibility to comb through his receipts to make sure he is not skimming the profits to pay for prostitutes or maintain his cocaine habit. But if you are this manager's district supervisor, and you have reason to know of such, you are indeed responsible and accountable. If you are a house-church member in Saudi Arabia, you are not responsible for your government's persecution of religious minorities. If you are part of the Saudi royal family, you certainly are. Pontius Pilate cannot claim at the Judgment Seat that his political decision to allow the execution of one alleged insurrectionist for the sake of the unity of the Empire should be inadmissible to the proceedings since it is a "political" or "social justice" question, nor can Herod do the same for his marriage since it was a "personal" matter.

God showed Elijah on that mountain that justice would be done, though such justice was yet in the future. At Naboth's vineyard, after the murder was accomplished, Elijah as mouthpiece for God pronounced a horrible verdict: "In the place where dogs licked up the blood of Naboth shall dogs lick your own blood" (1 Kings 21:19). He put forth a similar premonition about the end of Jezebel. Ahab responded with regret to this, putting on sackcloth and fasting, and so God delayed the coming judgment of him (1 Kings 21:27–29). This was, evidently from what we see in the pages following, not gospel repentance but a sort of temporary suspension of doom. Jezebel would still face her end.

This moment of confrontation with Ahab, like the earlier one over idolatry, was not just about the history as it unfolded at the time, but pointed forward to the future mission of Elijah, a mission he would not, in fact, live to carry out. One of the most fashionable spiritual beliefs of our time is in a sort of popularized and convoluted understanding of the Buddhist idea of karma, the belief that "what goes around comes around." To some degree, this is the way a secularized people cope with the loss of an idea of Judgment Day. But, in another way, this confused concept is partly right, rooted as it is in an intuition that sin and injustice are not, in fact, permanent realities—that somehow, one day, justice will be done. This is usually not done immediately, which is why, despite the fact that one of our most persistent theological questions is "why do good people suffer?" the reality is that just as often, maybe even more so, the question of injustice in people's hearts is exactly what it was in biblical times: "Why do the wicked prosper?"

By establishing the *what* of justice, though, God also here revealed to Elijah the *who*. Questions of justice in Scripture define not only *what* matters but *who* matters. That's why Jesus defined in his inaugural sermon not only God's content of the

"Day of the Lord"—of freedom for captives, sight for the blind, liberty for the oppressed—but also to whom this applied—not just to ethnic Israel but to Gentiles such as the widow of Zarephath or Naaman the Syrian (Luke 4:18–27). That's why Jesus defined for the self-justifying lawyer not only the content of what mercy is—loving neighbor as self in whatever way needed—but also the reframing of who that neighbor is—using the story of a despised Samaritan as the one who obeyed that command in caring for a man beaten by the side of the Jericho Road (Luke 10:25–37).

Likewise, here God moved quickly past the coming judgment of the house of Ahab right back to the concept of the remnant. God pointed not to success that would turn around the prophet's losing streak, but to that remnant: "Yet I will leave seven thousand in Israel, all the knees that have not bowed to Baal, and every mouth that has not kissed him" (1 Kings 19:18). This group of people were, at the moment, the most irrelevant factor in the whole equation. Elijah knew that he was not, in fact, the only one left. He knew that his fellow prophet Obadiah had hidden a hundred prophets in two caves, from Ahab and Jezebel (1 Kings 18:4).

While Elijah was not, like Ahab, persecuting the weakness of such a group, he evidently was not thinking of them at all. They, after all, did not have the influence to deal with the problem at hand. And no one would notice them if they were gone.

This is the exact dynamic at work in the Naboth situation to come. Ahab was, as Jezebel pointed out, the king of Israel. Who would notice if Naboth were gone? He was just an obstacle to be plowed over. But God saw and God knew. Again, most of us can see this in terms of the way we might imagine a king to act or, say, a wealthy man as in Jesus' parable of the rich man and Lazarus. But we often do not see the ways that our own failures to stand up for justice in our own lives often boil down to the question of what groups of people we value more than others, and what people we fear more than others.

But there's also included in God's revelation here about justice the question of *how*. God would use power—even the evil Hazael and the morally ambiguous Jehu—to turn Ahab's power-worship against him. Since he saw his own might as determinative of what is right and wrong, might would be what would take down his legacy. But the hope for the future was not with establishing some new dynasty for Jehu or Hazael. The hope was with the remnant. The hope for the future was with a group so irrelevant to the current discussion that Elijah did not even think to mention them.

This had to be disconcerting to Elijah. His lament, after all, was not just about the fate of the nation, but also about his own marginalization and coming execution. For him, the two were linked together. He, after all, was the bearer of God's word. And here God speaks of a future where he sets things right—but he does so by mentioning people other than Elijah. As a matter of fact, he explicitly revealed the name of the one who would take Elijah's place. God's word was irreplaceable, but Elijah was not. Elijah's exile to the wilderness was not, it turns out, about Ahab frustrating God's purpose. This *was* God's purpose for Elijah. Again, God was rescuing Elijah from going in the way of Ahab, by making his own relevance ultimate.

Earlier I mentioned how much easier it is to name children for prophets rather than kings, if one is looking for biblical names. As I wrote this it reminded me of the only time I have ever been embarrassed by my wife. We were visiting a new church, still adjusting to the newness of married life together, on a Sunday when the pastor was preaching on, I think, the opening chapters of Revelation, when he came to the risen Christ's identification of a false teacher as "Jezebel." Attempting to make a point about the ongoing notoriety of this evil Old Testament queen, the pastor said, "How many of you women are called 'Jezebel'? Raise your hand." My wife misheard him as saying, "How many of you women recall Jezebel?" She thought he was just gauging the familiarity of the crowd with the figure, not that he was asking who shared her name, so she raised her hand. "What are you doing?" I whispered, as I looked around the room, certain that, if we joined this church, people would be introducing us for years as "Russell and Jezebel Moore."

Later that day, the confusion morphed in my mind from humiliating to hilarious, especially because I know no one less similar to the Machiavellian murderess than my calm, gentle wife. Only later though, when we were able to laugh about the incident, did I really reflect on the fact that our sense of blushing at all that actually made the pastor's point. Not only is my wife not named Jezebel—I don't know anyone who is. Part of that is, of course, because most people who want to plumb the Bible for a name don't want a villain. But imagine someone who wanted a pagan name to pass on to a child. Someone who values the things Jezebel valued—fame, power, renown—also wouldn't want the name, for the same reason that even someone who didn't know that "Ichabod" means "the glory has departed" wouldn't want to name a child for the bumbling protagonist of *The Legend of Sleepy Hollow.*

Jezebel ended up repudiated and humiliated, even on her own terms. Jezebel, after all, gloried in her own significance. At her death, God saw to it that even this was removed. The Scripture says that when justice for her ultimately came, there was nothing left to bury of her except "the skull and the feet and the palms of her hands" (2 Kings 9:35). When told of this, Jehu remembered: "This is the word of the LORD, which he spoke by his servant Elijah the Tishbite: 'In the territory of Jezreel the dogs shall eat the flesh of Jezebel, and the corpse of Jezebel shall be as dung on the face of the field in the territory of Jezreel, so that no one can say, This is Jezebel'" (2 Kings 9:36–37). That is, to be sure, a gruesome picture. But that is where clinging to one's own relevance as an ultimate priority will lead—to destruction and to shame. Elijah's legacy, though, would come about in another way, through his replacement by others.

Elijah's exhaustion at seeing his work fail was not because the work was not worth doing, but because the work was so important that God would not allow it to be reduced to a "Baal" for Elijah himself. And the same will be true for you. Whatever mission in life God has called you toward—the rearing of children or the discipling of a small group or an evangelistic mission to a people group or the creation of capital for the care of the poor, whatever—God will usually see to it that most of what he does through you is invisible to you. Sometimes it will even look as though you are failing. That is often necessary for God to conform you to the image of the Christ who does not exalt himself but is the One who stands among others as the One who serves.

The priest Henri Nouwen wrote about how jarring it was for him to go from a place of celebrated ministry to serving in a home for developmentally disabled adults, who did not know who he was and were not the least bit impressed with his impressiveness in ministry. "These broken, wounded, and completely unpretentious people forced me to let go of my relevant self—the self that can do things, show things, prove things, build things, and forced me to reclaim that unadorned self in which I am completely vulnerable, open to receive and give love regardless of any accomplishments," he wrote. "I am telling you this because I am deeply convinced that the Christian leader of the future is called to be completely irrelevant and to stand in this world with nothing to offer but his or her own vulnerable self."[2]

This was true for Elijah. It was true for John. It will be true for you.

Reading through the New Testament it is striking that the only one who seems to lack a Messiah complex is, well, the actual Messiah. Almost everyone else, no matter how devoted to what is right, often put themselves at the center of accomplishing that right. God extricates the one from the other. In so doing, he frees us from the temptation toward apathy or toward participation in injustice. But he also frees us from the exhaustion that comes with seeing justice and righteousness as entirely dependent on us. Instead, we are free to ask, "What is right? What does God require of us in this moment?" and to also look around for the remnant, for where God may carry on our work without us. As Elder Zosima says in *The Brothers Karamazov:* "And if everyone abandons you and drives you out by force, then, when you are left alone, fall down on the earth and kiss it and water it with your tears, and the earth will bring forth fruit from your tears, even though no one has seen you or heard you in your solitude." And, as Zosima concludes: "Your work is for the whole; your deed is for the future."[3] The same was true for Elijah. He, as part of the fruit of that unseen remnant, was a testimony to that. And the same will be true for you. That's not the way of the hero. But it is the way of the disciple.

God's purpose of justice, and God's mysterious counter-intuitive ways of accomplishing it, remain part of Elijah's story, long past his exit. Remember that, in the closing chapters of the Old Testament, God spoke of a return of Elijah "before the great and awesome day of the LORD comes" (Mal. 4:5). This spirit of the prophet would come in the form of a messenger going on ahead of the Lord, announcing his coming. "And the Lord whom you seek will suddenly come to his temple" (Mal. 3:1). This is hardly, though, good news, in and of itself.

This coming would be one of a judgment on all the wickedness done in his name. "But who can endure the day of his coming, and who can stand when he appears?" Malachi asked (Mal. 3:2). This judgment would be for those things we might characterize as "vertical" (wrong ways of worshipping God; idolatry) and those things that we might classify as "horizontal" (mistreatment of neighbor). And those "horizontal" questions of judgment include both those things some would classify as "personal morality" and those things some would call "social justice" issues: "I will be a swift witness against the sorcerers, against the adulterers, against those who swear falsely, against those who oppress the hired worker in his wages, the widow and the fatherless, against those who thrust aside the sojourner, and do not fear me, says the LORD of hosts" (Mal. 3:5).

God closed out his first covenant revelation by reminding his people that they could not find places to work immorality or injustice that are cordoned off from his scrutiny. Indeed, to do so would be to make the mistake the Syrian army made against Israel in the days of Elijah, to conclude that, "The LORD is a god of the hills but he is not a god of the valleys" (1 Kings 20:28). And yet, the final word is not one of judgment but of a reconciliation that comes out of the judgment. The spirit of Elijah would ultimately bring about a "vertical" reconciliation (salvation from destruction) and a "horizontal" reconciliation ("he will turn the hearts of fathers to their children and the hearts of children to their fathers"), both of these (Mal. 4:6).

And this is precisely what happened. Jesus came into the temple, and turned over tables, driving out the moneychangers. This was because of both the "vertical" aspect of a compromise of the holiness of worship ("My house shall be called a house of prayer") and the "horizontal" aspect of mistreatment of those invisible at the moment ("for all nations"). Reflecting on this perplexing incident, Jesus' disciples remember the phrase from the Psalms, "Zeal for your house will consume me" (John 2:17; Ps. 69:9). That is literally something like, "Zeal for your house will tear me to pieces." And, of course, it did.

The charge that Jesus was setting out to destroy the temple was one of the allegations made leading to his crucifixion. And yet, in that crucifixion, Jesus accomplished the very thing he promised. The temple—of his body—was torn down, and in three days he built it back up again. And in that temple, made of living stones connecting heaven to earth, he embodies worship of God, holiness of life, love of God and of neighbor, and the reconciliation of people to God and to each other. In that new reality, we learn what it is that God requires of a reborn people: "to do justice, and to love kindness, and to walk humbly with your God" (Mic. 6:8). The zeal that led Elijah to exhaustion is what led Jesus to crucifixion, and then beyond it to a new creation.

Injustice arouses the wrath of God. The reconciling power of God, though, creates us into a people who reflect the priorities of Jesus himself (Ps. 72:1–14). That means that we will have a long-term view of what matters and who matters. And we will not be afraid of so-called "losing causes." As those reconciled to God, we can see both Creation and Fall, and we know that the Fall is not the end of the story, nor is it the beginning.

People are created in the image of God and endowed by him with certain unalienable rights, of that Mr. Jefferson was quite right. All people were also endowed with consciences carrying messages from that Creator. In moments when guards are down, people can perceive the goodness of creation, the dignity of their neighbors, the inevitability of an accounting for our lives (Rom. 2:15–16). And so we stand and speak for those the world doesn't want to hear about—the neglected, abused women, unborn children, scapegoated migrants, and persecuted religious minorities—not because we are necessarily "winning" on the issue at the moment, but because we are bearing witness to something, to Someone, larger than the moment. A sense of God's providence and sovereignty keeps us from despair. A sense of the human Fall and the spiritual war around us keeps us from triumphalism. In holding both together, we see the City of God and the City of Man together, one hurtling toward death but the other marching to Zion.

Some of those killing the Naboths around them, and annexing the vineyards, may well be turned around. Sometimes these are the very ones who lead in the cause for justice and dignity and reconciliation later on. Others will not. But whether we "win" or "lose" in the short-term, we see the full picture. And it's a vision of God's justice and mercy to which he calls us to participate, but which will move on with or without us.

Zeal is necessary, but zeal is not enough. The zeal must lead us to self-sacrifice. The zeal must lead us to a cross-shaped justice and a cross-shaped gospel that is willing to be thought strange and irrelevant, that is willing to be ridiculed and forgotten, as long as the voice one is following into the darkness is the voice we have heard before, the voice that says "Come, follow me."

Somewhere in Alabama, there's a shuttered church that used to thrive. But it could not see the difference between the kingdom of God and southern culture, between the body of Christ and the White Citizens' Council. The gospel, however, moved on without it and, as in the rest of the world, the mission is carried out by people who would have been excluded by that church in its heyday. As a matter of fact, most of the gathered crowd around the throne in Revelation 5 would have been excluded from membership, as would have the dark-skinned, non-English-speaking Middle Easterner sitting on the throne in the midst of that scene. You might say he was already excluded a long time ago. To stand for justice would have meant being strange and odd and "ineffective" in the moment, and so the church chose its relevance over what was right. I wonder how many of us do the same. That's where fear can lead. But faith leads us elsewhere, toward the courage to stand for what is right.

The arc of history is long, but it bends toward Jesus.

# Chapter Eight

# Courage and the Future

## *Meaning through Mystery*

A night light shines in the darkness of the hallway at my house. It's not to help me to see in the dark. It's there to remind me that I already can. This night light is in the shape of a wardrobe, and pictures young Lucy standing there at the door into the snows of Narnia. The light shines out from the stars overhead and from the lamppost there in the center. When I see that night light, I am reminded of how those stories helped lead me out of my own time of deep, deep darkness. It glows with familiarity for me. But it burns with mystery too. After all, I know where Lucy is going—to Mr. Tumnus's house, to the Stone Table, on to Cair Paravel, and then to the truer, greater

Narnia. But, at this point in the story, she doesn't know all of that. At this moment, frozen in that scene, she knows nothing of witches or lions or fauns. There's just a lamppost and a winter sky. There's just a light shining in the darkness. And when I started out on my own trek through the dark woods, I could not see where I was going either, and could not have named precisely what was beckoning me onward. The same may well be true for you. And maybe that's why you are afraid.

Indeed, much of what we fear is not so much because we do not think that we can endure what scares us. Most of us have seen people who have done just that. Much of our fear is rooted in mystery, that we do not know what is around the corner from us. We cannot see how everything is going to turn out for us. Sitting around a fireplace with some friends one night, one of them posed the conversation-starter: "If you could have one thing—past, present, or future—that you could read right now what would it be?" I think he answered his own question that he would want to read whatever Jesus wrote with his fingers in the sand at the attempted stoning of the woman caught in adultery, words that caused the would-be executioners to drop their stones and walk away.

Without even thinking, I said, "My obituary."

One in our number winced and said, "Good grief, Moore, that's kind of dark." But as I explained why I would want to look into the future and see that obituary, I realized that what I was indulging was not my curiosity but my fear.

If I could read that obituary, I would know, first of all, exactly when I would die. If the date were tomorrow, I would immediately go home and stay up all night with my wife and children. If that date were forty years from now, with my cause of death reported as a shark attack, I might be nervous to swim in murky waters for the rest of my life, but I would have no anxiety at all crossing busy streets or wondering what that persistent headache means. I would know, after all, that a shark was going to kill me—not a stroke, not a heart attack, not a brain tumor, and not an oncoming bus. Until that forty years was up, I would be invincible. But that would not be the most important part of that obituary for me.

Before I even looked for the date or cause of death, I would look for the line started with the words "He is survived by . . ." I would hold my breath until I could see that my wife's name was there, along with all of my children. I would want to decipher all sorts of mysteries. Do my sons have spouses' names listed? Do they have children of their own? I would try to read into their responsibilities at my funeral the answer to the questions about this future time line. Do they still love me? Were they proud of me? Did my life make any difference for them? Even as I worked through that thought experiment, I was shaken to see just how much it revealed about my skewed priorities right now. I noticed that I really did not care what strangers thought of me. What I cared about was this woman and these sons. So why do strangers' opinions or approval matter so much to me now, when I will go to my grave with it making not one bit of difference to me?

My friend is right. The thought experiment is kind of morbid. But the reason I would want to see that obituary is because I would want to decipher the meaning of my life. I would want to see how the story ends, in order to see how the plotline resolves. If I knew how all that worked out, I would be afraid of nothing. The reason this is the case is because an obituary is not just a collection of data. An obituary, if one knows how to read it, is a story. And it is a story with an origin narrative and a resolved plotline. It is an attempt, however small, to make meaning out of a life at the one point where one can finally see it all—after it is over. In a very real sense, that's what we spend our entire lives trying to do. That is what courage is about.

After his own trek through the wilderness, Elijah was given no glimpse of his own obituary. God did indeed unveil something of the future, but all of that was about his own judgment against evil, and about the ultimate triumph of God's mercy through the remnant. The success of God's mission was forecast, but not, specifically, what would happen to Elijah, except that Elijah was to recruit his own replacement.

When Elijah found Elisha, Elisha asked to have time to say goodbye to his parents. This is hardly an unreasonable request, which is why it is so shocking when Jesus refuses his own disciples the opportunity to do the same (Luke 9:57–62). Afterward Elisha sacrificed the oxen with which he was plowing. This hardly means much to most modern readers, since fewer and fewer people are around livestock, much less animal sacrifices. But this act was not just an ancient rite for Elisha. These were the oxen with which he had been plowing. His sacrificing them was the offering up of not just some beasts of burden, but of his entire story of self up to that point—his livelihood, his inheritance, the hopes his family had for him, his expectations of the future. Elisha was sacrificing his story for a future that was, to him, a mystery.

As the Bible moves along, Elijah was, as usual, a mystery to those who pursued him: appearing from nowhere, disappearing into obscurity, calling down fire from heaven, speaking the oracles of God. But, all along, God was leading Elijah somewhere that was increasingly looking to be his end. As Elisha followed along, he asked for only one thing: a double anointing of the Spirit of God that rested on the old prophet. Elijah said that God would grant that request only if Elisha were to see the final end of Elijah, of his moment of glory. And, of course, that's precisely what happened. Elisha watched as Elijah was taken away in a whirlwind, with chariots of fire and horses of flame appearing alongside (2 Kings 2:11).

And as he sees this uncanny vision, Elisha cries out "My father, my father!" (2 Kings 2:12). This language of father to son is crucial. The relationship between parents and children, after all, does not just assure us that there's a future but that we have a planned obsolescence. From parents to children, we decrease as they increase. We hand off the future to them. And that can be unsettling. A friend once lamented the fact that he thought he was losing his youthful looks as he aged. "I look like somebody's dad," he said. Another friend looked at him and said, flatly, "You *are* somebody's dad." The sort of handoff from fathers to sons, from mothers to daughters, is not just a matter of biology, and not just a matter of extraordinary epoch-defining prophetic succession. This is part of everyday discipleship. Naomi is a mother to Ruth (Ruth 1:11–18), Paul a father to Timothy (1 Tim. 1:2). And in both of these cases, the parental figures clearly saw their own stories ending, as they continued in another. That's difficult for a fallen humanity, in which we want to see ourselves as self-generating, self-sustaining, and virtually immortal, in which we don't want to think that we will be surpassed.

Often a young minister will tell me excitedly of a new opportunity to serve alongside an older pastor, nearing retirement, with the arrangement that, after some unspecified time, the pastor will step aside and turn over the reins to the younger. This is almost always a disaster. Except in cases of remarkable maturity, the typical pattern is that the older leader starts to view the younger as a sign of his mortality. If he has tied his own sense of self-worth and meaning to his work, he ends up resenting this interloper the way a person with a persistent cough would resent a neighbor standing on his front lawn each night dressed as the Grim Reaper.

That can happen in any venue of life, not just in ministry. We so often see the same scenario working itself out in the church just as much as in Silicon Valley or on Wall Street or at the office supply chain store down the street—with one generation throwing spears at the next. We can tell ourselves this is because of "the cause" or "our concerns" when really what's enraging us is hearing "Saul has killed his thousands and David his tens of thousands." We are scared not so much of dying as of being eclipsed and forgotten. We are scared that our lives will not have had meaning.

Elijah was not, so far as we can see, hostile to the next generation in his life, but he was oblivious to that remnant—even when he knew about a hundred of them hidden in caves. He just did not seem attentive to that development in the story. By the end, though, Elijah is not only blessing and handing over his life's work to a son in the faith, but he is doing so preparing to be outdone by that protégé.

The Bible makes clear that this is precisely what God intended. Immediately after seeing Elijah raptured away, Elisha put on the old man's mantle, came to the water's edge and said, "Where is the LORD, the God of Elijah?" The waters parted, just as they had for Elijah, just as they had for their forefathers at the Exodus (2 Kings 2:14). And Elisha knew the right question to ask. The others wanted to know, "Where is Elijah?" They sent out search parties seeking him out for three days, but his whereabouts remained a mystery. Elisha though knew that the question was not where Elijah was, but where Elijah's God was. He was there. And the rest of the biblical account at this point shows us Elisha stepping right into the Elijah story—carrying out the mission Elijah was given in the wilderness (2 Kings 8:10–15; 9:1–13). God had de-centered Elijah from his own story. And in order to do that, God ensured that Elijah would know what he did not know in the wilderness, how to answer that question, "What are you doing here, Elijah?" And the right answer is, "I do not know."

Notice the contrast between the journey of Elijah (from that mountain in his 1 Kings 19 crisis all the way through to his explosion of glory) and that of the royal house. Despite the death of Ahab, it seems as though judgment would not really clear the scene. The Baals were still present. When Ahab's successor Ahaziah suffers a humiliating injury, falling through the lattice on his rooftop, and his health is desperate, he doubled down on the idolatry. Like all of us, the king wanted one piece of information to endure what he was going through: "Is this going to be all right in the end?" So he sent messengers to another foreign deity "Baal-zebub," literally "the Lord of the flies," for a sign. He sought to see whether he would face death by inquiring of a god of decay and gore. This is more than just a wrongful act of worship (though that would be bad enough). Jesus later would be accused of casting out demons by "Beelzebul," the lord of the flies (Luke 11:14–19).

This attempt by the king to peer into his future by some other means than the revelation of God was, like Saul with the Witch of Endor before him, satanic to the core. And it was also counter-productive. As Jesus would later note, the house of Beelzebul would be plundered, as that strong man was overcome and bound by the power of the crucified. Elijah, on the other hand, was no longer the whining, inquiring person he was before. He simply followed the light given, bit by bit by bit, as it led him along to another mountain, where, unlike before, God would, in fact, be in the whirlwind.

Now, most of us do not face the temptation to seek out occultists to tell us our futures (though some, of course, do). But we face the exact same temptation in another way. What is unknown scares us, and we want to know where we are headed ahead of time, so that we can be sure that we can handle whatever might come our way. We want to put ourselves out of our mystery. For most of us, this is done not by seeking out witches but by worry. Worrying, after all, often is a turning over and over again in our heads of various future scenarios, with the illusion that if we ponder these possible futures enough we can somehow gain power over them. Jesus taught us to be "anxious for nothing," not only because worry could do nothing to change tomorrow but also because the sort of "thought for tomorrow" that worry is actually distracts us from both our present reality—God's ongoing care seen in the flourishing of sparrows and lilies of the field—and our future goal—the kingdom of God (Matt. 6:33).

Jesus tells us a bit about our near-term futures—that they will be filled with sorrows and rejections and persecutions— and our long-term futures—that we will reign with him over the cosmos (Luke 22:29). But he does not tell us much. Indeed, a critical part of the formation to serve in the kingdom to come is a sense of mystery, of learning to walk by faith not by sight (2 Cor. 5:7), to see the kingdom ahead through a glass darkly (1 Cor. 13:12). That sense of mystery in the life of Elijah continued to the end and beyond his exit in the whirlwind.

Where did he go? What was he doing there? Would he be coming back? No one knew. All that was left was his cloak. That's why some of the new generation of prophets concluded that maybe he was dropped off on some mountain or into a ravine, and that they should rescue him (2 Kings 2:17). That was not unreasonable, since Elijah had, as we have seen, been lost in the wilds, near death before. Were he paying attention to the actions on this side of the veil of glory, old Elijah might have muttered, "Where was your search party when I needed it?" But they found nothing (2 Kings 2:17). Like Moses before him, whose grave could not be found, Elijah was cloaked in even more mystery—no one knew if he was even alive. He was just gone. Though his spirit marched forward from Elisha to John the Baptist, and though his name rustled through the leaves of the Bible to come, we do not see Elijah—until a thousand years later. And that moment of mystery uncovers precisely what you need to find the courage to stand.

What Elisha saw beyond the Jordan was almost inexpressible: a whirlwind into heaven and chariots of fire. The oddness of it all is why secularists of all sorts have dismissed it as some sort of myth, while some conspiracy theorists have seen it as evidence of an ancient alien abduction. But the imagery here is consistent with what the Bible will define elsewhere as an unveiling. Elisha was able to see in Elijah's departure a thin place in the border between the spiritual and material worlds. This is not the only time that such would happen.

Later in the life of Elisha, he would find himself along with a servant surrounded by Syrian armies. The younger man panicked. But Elisha said, "Do not be afraid, for those who are with us are more than those who are with them" (2 Kings 6:16).

The servant had every reason to wonder whether his mentor was insane. Like Elijah back in the desert, he could see that they were outnumbered and that their doom was approaching. Elisha asked of God that the young man's eyes would be opened "that he may see" (2 Kings 6:17). At that moment, "he saw, and behold, the mountain was full of horses and chariots of fire all around Elisha" (2 Kings 2:17). Notice that Elisha did not summon these chariots of fire. They were already there. He simply allowed, for one blinding moment, this scared youth to see what was already surrounding them in the spiritual arena. And what he saw was what the Bible will elsewhere call "glory."

In the Gospels, Jesus was teaching his disciples that "the Son of Man is going to come with his angels in the glory of his Father, and then he will repay each person according to what he has done" (Matt. 16:27). But, even more shockingly, Jesus said, "Truly, I say to you, there are some standing here who will not taste death until they see the Son of Man coming in his kingdom" (Matt. 16:28). Six days later, Jesus took the central core of his disciples—Peter, James, and John—up a high mountain by themselves. Just as Elisha had his anointing dependent on whether he "saw" the glory of Elijah's departure, they were told they would "see" the glory of Jesus' arrival. And on that mountain, something happened: "he was transfigured before them, and his face shone like the sun, and his clothes became white as light" (Matt. 17:2).

Those who had been "standing there" earlier were standing no more: they fell on their faces. They saw a bright cloud overshadowing everything around them, and they saw a conversation happening—their Rabbi with Moses and Elijah. Once again, we have no indication that anything changed on that mountain, other than what Peter, James, and John were allowed to see. They saw a universe alive with the radiance of God, with unseen spiritual realities, with a cloud of witnesses that are not nearly as dead as we think they are. They saw a glimpse of glory.

C. S. Lewis wrote that "glory" suggests two things: applause and glowing light, and he conceded that both of these seem a bit ridiculous at first glance. "As for the first, since to be famous means to be better known than other people, the desire for fame appears to be a competitive passion and therefore of hell rather than heaven," he wrote. "As for the second, who wishes to become a kind of living electric light bulb?"[1] But as he explored further, he came to see that this is precisely what all of us long for—a sense of approval, a sense of being seen. Think, for instance, of the person who walks out onto the field at an empty athletic stadium and imagines the lights focused on him, with the crowds chanting his name; or, the person who fantasizes about standing in the spotlight singing, with the audience applauding her uproariously. Yes, this is grandiosity of a soul-sick kind, but where does it originate? What in our createdness is twisted toward this end?

Both of these elements of glory were present on the Mount of Transfiguration. There was dazzling brilliance of a supernatural sort—what the Eastern church would call "uncreated light"—and there was the voice of God, thundering out once again that this was his beloved Son, with whom he was well pleased. This vision of glory was significant with the company assembled, since both Moses and Elijah were defined by glimpses of glory. Moses, of course, begged of God, "Please show me your glory" and was hidden in the cleft of a rock as the glory passed him by (Exod. 33:18–22). After meeting with God on Mount Sinai, Moses' face was shining with secondhand light to the point that the prophet was forced to wear a veil to keep the people from being overwhelmed by it. And Elijah, of course, had called down fire from heaven, had been borne away into heaven with manifestations of glory. Here, in the presence of Jesus, they saw the glory of God that they had longed for, that they had seen shattered glimpses of, in person. This Jesus of Nazareth is, the Bible reveals, "the radiance of the glory of God and the exact imprint of his nature, and he upholds the universe by the word of his power" (Heb. 1:3).

This might seem distant from your own life, but it is not. You, if you are a follower of Jesus, have been to that mountain also. The glory that Moses and Elijah saw was not some impersonal afterglow of the presence of God. That glory was, in fact, the person of Jesus Christ. Another prophet, Isaiah, would famously see the glory of God filling up the temple, both the radiance and the voice (Isa. 6:1–6). This passage is often preached in churches, around missions campaigns, since it culminates with "Here I am, send me" (Isa. 6:8). But what we often do not hear is that this glory was not a "What" but a "Who." John—one of the witnesses of Transfiguration glory—wrote that, "Isaiah said these things because he saw his glory and spoke of him," the "him" being Jesus (John 12:41). John, this eyewitness, wrote "We have seen his glory, glory as of the only Son of the Father, full of grace and truth" (John 1:14). This was, of course, a rattling and memorable "beholding" of that glory. But John wrote that this was not the only time he saw it. The occasion of Jesus turning water to wine at the wedding in Cana, for instance, "manifested his glory" (John 2:11).

To see Jesus is to see the glory of God. To hear Jesus is to hear the glory of God. And you, if you are a follower of Christ, have done both. The apostle Paul wrote that the glory of God is present in the hearing and believing of the gospel message, and that this glory does not fade away, like what Moses had seen, but that it transfigures the one who approaches. "And we all, with unveiled face, beholding the glory of the Lord, are being transformed into the same image from one degree of glory to another" (2 Cor. 3:18). The light that shines forth in the gospel, the light that frees us from the power of the Devil, is "the light of the gospel of the glory of Christ, who is the image of God"

(2 Cor. 4:4). That glory in our lives, just as it was for the disciples except for that one brief moment, just as it was for Elijah and Elisha and Moses, except for those momentary fragments, is impossible to see except through faith.

Here is why this matters for you, as you move toward courage. Although I agree with Lewis that glory speaks of luminosity and applause, I would add that both of these point to something else: to the resolution of a storyline. Glory, after all, is not a crystallized and timeless abstraction in the Bible, but a plot. The glory of God goes with Israel out of Egypt and into the land of promise, housed in tabernacles. The glory of God falls into Solomon's temple, where the glory resides, until the glory dramatically departs at the exile. The glory of God is promised to return, that the entire earth "will be filled with the knowledge of the glory of the LORD as the waters cover the sea" (Hab. 2:14). The glory is not just a thing, but the control-plot of the entire cosmic story.

The novelist Reynolds Price noted that storytelling emerged out of a profound human need for consolation and companionship. We can see that even in the way that, when faced with disaster (be it a personal disaster or a geopolitical one), most of us turn to some form of storytelling—whether in books or film or some other medium. But, Price argued, this "hunger" is more than just a biological and cultural adaptation. "The need is not for the total consolation of narcotic fantasy—our own will performed in airless triumph—but for credible news that our lives proceed in order toward a pattern which, if tragic here and now, is ultimately pleasing in the mind of a god who sees a totality and *at last* enacts His will," Reynolds wrote. "We crave nothing less than perfect story; and while we chatter or listen all our lives in a din of craving—jokes, anecdotes, novels, dreams, films, plays, songs, half the words of our days—we are satisfied only by the one short tale we feel to be true: *History is the will of a just god who knows us*" (emphasis his).[2]

His point is not just that we need a storyline to make sense of life, but that we need that story to be outside of us. As one philosopher put it, "an action is always an episode in a possible history." This means that even our notions of morality and justice and meaning only happen if we see an endpoint toward which our individual and collective stories are moving. Without this, this philosopher argues, people are "unscripted, anxious stutterers in their actions as in their words."[3] And that means accountability to a story that runs from birth to death, interlocking with the stories of others, to live, in his words, "a narratable life."[4] This demands not only a personal God, but also a Day of Judgment and a definition of glory.

When God lit up Jesus with heavenly light, conferring upon him his unqualified approval, God was revealing something about the Mystery holding everything together. Much of what scared Elijah in the desert and on the mountain was not just that his life would come to an end, by the hand of Jezebel, but that his life would have no meaning. God never showed him how it was to be otherwise. On Mount Horeb, Elijah heard a barely audible voice. On the Mount of Transfiguration, Elijah heard a voice unmistakable in its clarity, centered on Jesus of Nazareth, and saying unequivocally: "He is the point of it all."

This moment had to be disorienting. And one can count on, when disoriented, poor old Simon Peter saying something stupid. The Gospel of Mark records, "And Peter said to Jesus, 'Rabbi, it is good that we are here. Let us make three tents, one for you and one for Moses and one for Elijah,'" before adding, in an aside that always makes me chuckle: "For he did not know what to say, for they were terrified" (Mark 9:5–6). To be fair, anyone would be terrified, and short of words. And, moreover, what Peter said only seems stupid to us because it was rebuked by the voice of God.

On its own, Peter's suggestion makes a great deal of sense. Something momentous had happened there, something that Peter offered to memorialize. Beyond that, Peter probably wanted to honor the two greatest prophets of our history as the people of God, both of whom were not memorialized with graves. Moses was taken up to a high mountain and looked out at the land of promise, but could not enter it. He was buried in foreign territory "but no one knows the place of his burial to this day" (Deut. 34:6). Elijah could not be found by a search party, which was in frantic pursuit of him for three days, but it was promised he would come back, right before the end of everything. And here he was. Here they both were. Peter wanted monuments to try to make some meaning out of this mystery.

"He was still speaking when, behold, a bright cloud over-shadowed them, and a voice from the cloud said, 'This is my beloved Son, with whom I am well pleased; listen to him'" (Matt. 17:5). Their reactions were manifestly human: "When the disciples heard this, they fell on their faces and were terrified. But Jesus came and touched them, saying, 'Rise and have no fear'" (Matt. 17:6–7). It is the next line that is the key to this entire account: "And when they lifted up their eyes, they saw no one but Jesus only" (Matt. 17:8). I believe it is no accident that one of these disciples, John, when writing about the glory of Christ, alluded to the Word become flesh "dwelling" among us, in wording that suggests a tabernacle (John 1:14). God was saying to Simon Peter: "You don't need to make a house for me; I am making a house for you, and there he is." And God was also saying, "No monument is needed for Moses and Elijah. The Law and the Prophets are here to bear witness to him. Jesus is the one who makes sense of them."

Elijah was not the point. He was there only basking in reflected glory. And, in fact, that's the only sort of glory he had ever known or ever would know. The mystery of Elijah's life would not, despite his best efforts, be defined for him on Mount

Horeb. It would be defined for him on a different mountain, in the face of a Galilean carpenter.

Now, again, this comes back to the mystery of your own life. While you probably rarely think of "glory" by name, this is actually what you see as the endpoint: the sign that everything is going to work out all right in the end. The "light" tells you what was in the darkness, that you are safe. The applause tells you that you are approved of, that your life had significance. The glory is the endpoint that makes meaning out of the middle of your story.

Years ago, I found myself, incredibly, at the dinner table with an author whose books helped me through many difficult points in my life. He was a hero from afar and, like Simon Peter, my awe led to bumbling and mumbling as I tried to tell him how much his work had meant to me, while not acting like a star-struck "fan." This old man just smiled and said, "Isn't it something how we get exactly what we need, exactly when we need it? The right book comes along at just the right time. The right conversation happens at just the right time. The right friends come to us, just when we need them." He smiled and was quiet for a minute and said, "Haven't you noticed that in your life? It's grace, that's what it is." He said those words to me, it turns out, at just the right time. I've thought about them often in the years since, looking back at people and books and conversations that I did not know at the time were meaningful, but they changed everything.

"Writing novels I got into the habit of looking for plots," wrote another author who changed a lot of things for me, Frederick Buechner. "After awhile, I began to suspect that my own life had a plot. And after awhile more, I began to suspect that life itself has a plot."[5] That does not mean, he suggests, that our lives find their meaning in the dramatic and the radical, in those sharp moments when we clearly know that our whole lives will be different from then on, but in those ordinary, humdrum, even boring moments that shape a plotline of grace in our lives. He writes: "You get married, a child is born or not born, in the middle of the night there is a knocking at the door, on the way home through the park you see a man feeding pigeons, all the tests come in negative and the doctor gives you your life again: incident follows incident helter-skelter leading apparently nowhere, but then once in a while there is the suggestion of purpose, meaning, direction, the suggestion of plot, the suggestion that, however clumsily, your life is trying to tell you something, to take you somewhere."[6]

This "listening to your life," though, is not the sort of individualistic self-centeredness that we see in much of the "spirituality" around us (and in us). One can always draw a crowd of people by teaching them how to "pursue destiny," usually in terms of their money, their health, or their relationships. One can see people do this with their jobs or their love interests by telling themselves, "I was born for this." That's not, though, how Jesus identifies and informs meaning in our lives. As a matter of fact, most of the time, the specifics of our life's meaning are hidden from us in mystery. And that is what we mean when we say that life has a plot, rather than an easily-discerned "moral of the story." A plot is not just a series of facts, but an interplay of intelligibility and mystery.

The novelist E. M. Forster put it this way: "'the king dies and then the queen died' is a story; 'The king dies, and then the queen died of grief' is a plot." He corrected himself by further suggesting that even closer to the idea of plot would be, "The queen died, no one knew why, until it was discovered that it was through grief at the death of the king."[7] This interplay of intelligibility and mystery is resonant with our own experience of the cosmos. The more we know about the universe—the laws of physics, the existence of black holes, and so on—the more we realize how little we know. What is the mysterious "dark matter" that makes up most of the universe, but which none of us can define? The same is true of our own lives.

This can be disorienting to any one of us, as we walk into the darkness of our futures. Elijah was in anguish about the mystery of his own future as he trekked out into the wilderness. He could only see the meaning of it all, fully, here in the presence of the glory of a transfigured Christ. He is not alone. And what Elijah had learned back in his exile experience is what Peter, James, and John would learn as well—the meaning of a life is not in monuments or memorials but in conformity to Christ—and that alone. The reason the Mount of Transfiguration is so important to the Elijah story is because here we see what God was doing in that climactic plot-pivot in the wilderness. He was decentering Elijah from his own story. And that is what God will do for you and for me as well.

This was seen in down-payment form in the handover of mission to Elisha, in the fact that God would speak of his long-term plans while not disclosing Elijah's own short-term fate. But it is seen ever clearer in the way that John the Baptist inherited the spirit of Elijah. The apostle John—one of those who witnessed this explosion into light on the mountain— opened his Gospel describing Jesus as the light that has come into the world. And then the apostle wrote: "There was a man sent from God, whose name was John. He came as a witness, to bear witness about the light, that all might believe through him. *He was not the light* but came to bear witness to the light" (John 1:6–8, emphasis mine). Not only does the apostle tell us this as narrator, he also pictured the Baptist himself making just that point. One of the first questions he received was "Who are you?" and his answer is instructive. He said, "I am not the Christ" (John 1:20). They kept asking, "What then? Are you Elijah?" (John 1:21), and his answer was again no. "So they said to him, 'Who are you? We need to give an answer to those who sent us. What do you say about yourself?'" (John 1:22). The mystery of this life had to be resolved. And so John the Baptist said, "I am the voice of one crying out in the wilderness, 'Make straight the way of the Lord,' as the prophet Isaiah said" (John 1:23).

Sooner or later, in the quest for meaning, one must grapple with that question, "Who are you?" And usually what we mean by that question is something like, "Once I get beyond the expectations other people have of me, beyond the roles that I play and the jobs that I have, who am I really, down at my core?" That's not a bad question to ask, but it's a bad *first* question to ask. On its own, that question is unanswerable. First, we must learn, as did John, to confess what we are *not* before we can say what we *are*. John was learning what Elijah had learned before him: "He must increase, but I must decrease" (John 3:30). This, not the diet of insects nor the garment of hair, was the most Elijah-like thing about John the Baptist. Elijah learned that, with clarity, in the wilderness, where he was led to surrender his own storyline that he might find it in another.

Elijah started out speaking of himself as a servant of the God "before whom I stand." And then Elijah came to stand in silence at the mouth of a cave, waiting for a word from God about his life and future. But here on this mountain, Elijah saw the fire from heaven, heard the voice from God—but it was all about Jesus, not about Elijah. The cloud of that glory "over-shadowed" Elijah and the others, in more ways than one. And when the cloud of glory lifted, Jesus was the last man standing.

And so it is with you. That is why the Transfiguration is situated in the story where it is. This moment of glory—with celebrity guests and all—comes between two meditations on the cross. Jesus telling his disciples that some of them would not taste death until they had seen his glory was in the context of telling them something far graver. "If anyone would come after me, let him deny himself and take up his cross and follow me," Jesus said. "For whoever would save his life will lose it, but whoever loses his life for my sake will find it" (Matt. 16:24–25). That the glory and the cross go together is clear even in the Transfiguration itself. Elijah, along with Moses, "appeared in glory" with Jesus, and there they "spoke of his departure, which he was about to accomplish at Jerusalem" (Luke 9:31). Elijah on his own mountain of turmoil was concerned about whether he would live or die. But here, in glory on this mountain, Elijah is focused only on the cross. The disciples of Jesus certainly wanted to save their own lives. That is why Peter rebuked Jesus for even suggesting that he would be arrested and killed. But they were fitting themselves into the wrong story.

On the way down the mountain, after Elijah was gone, the disciples wanted to talk about Elijah. Why, they asked, "do the scribes say that first Elijah must come?" (Matt. 17:10). Jesus answered: "Elijah does come, and he will restore all things. But I tell you that Elijah has already come, and they did not recognize him, but did whatever they pleased. So also the Son of Man will certainly suffer at their hands" (Matt. 17:11–12). The disciples knew he was speaking of John the Baptist, and they must have shuddered. They knew how that story had ended.

After all, John, like Elijah, faced down his own Ahab and Jezebel—the king Herod and Herodias (the "they" that Jesus mentioned, declining to even honor them with the very thing their egocentric reigns most desired: the remembrance of their names). John told Herod just what Elijah had told Ahab: that he was accountable to God, and that just because he wanted something (in Ahab's case, a peasant's vineyard and in Herod's case a brother's wife) did not mean he could have it. And he ended up executed. The "voice crying in the wilderness" ended up a severed voice box on a silver platter. The mouth that had spoken "Behold the Lamb of God who takes away the sin of the world" was taken out with the trash.

But the astounding aspect of this story was not in the gore or violence, but in the final words of the account. The followers of John "took the body and buried it, and they went and told Jesus" (Matt. 14:12). Those words fit the entire event—not just the murder of John but his entire life—in the right plotline, in the plotline of Jesus. There were, after all, two kingdoms there: one obvious, with a palace address and an entourage, and one hidden—moving imperceptibly, like yeast through a loaf of bread. One empire would fall in disgrace, and the other would rise in glory. But that would happen by the way of the cross. That's where Elijah found the meaning of his life, his glory, and it's also where you must find yours.

The poet Christian Wiman writes that the world is divided between those who think that all of reality holds together and those who think there's a "crack that runs through creation." The first group then seeks to conform themselves to this unity, and the second seeks to repair what is broken, or to resist what is awful. He writes that both are true, which means that human life must include both awe and horror. "I believe the right response to reality is to bow down, and I believe the right response to reality is to scream," he writes. "Life is tragic and faith is comic."[8] This paradox is right at the core of any right reading of the world. As the songwriter Leonard Cohen famously expressed it, "There is a crack in everything; that's how the light gets in."[9] The cross makes sense of both that awe-inspiring integrity of the universe, and the scandal of its brokenness. It's where the glory of God—seen in that brief moment on the mountain—converges with our own tragic stories. The cross is precisely how you find courage, because in the crucified Christ you find your future, with both your worst- and best-case scenarios. The head you lose may be your own. That's not the end of the world.

When it comes to fighting fear, some counsel "positive thinking," where a person imagines only the good things that can happen, under the assumption that thinking this way can will those things into existence. Others—from the ancient Stoics to some modern cognitive behavioral therapists—would suggest that the reverse is the best course, to ask when facing something scary: "What is the worst thing that could happen?" Even more liberating though is to be on the other side of your worst-case scenario—to see that it did happen, and that you survived. That's what has happened to you, if you are a follower of Jesus.

The worst thing that can happen to you is not torture by Ahab or exile by Jezebel or beheading by Herod. Elijah survived all of that and, ultimately, John did too. The worst thing that can happen to you is not whatever you are worried about right now—your spouse leaving you, your employer firing you, your child getting addicted, your doctor telling you that you have an inoperable tumor. The worst thing that can possibly happen to you is hell, being cut off from the presence of God, condemned under the curse of the Law. If you are in Christ, then you are crucified with him (Gal. 2:20). That means your worst-case scenario has already happened, and can never be repeated.

Moreover, your best-case scenario is also right in front of you. Your best-case scenario, if you are in Christ, is not your dream job or your dream spouse or your dream family or a long, healthy life dying in your bed with a smile on your face. Your best-case scenario is exactly what the disciples saw on that mountain: glory, a glory that never fades and that goes on forever. That has happened too. Jesus is raised from the dead, seated at the right hand of God in the heavenly places (Eph. 1:20–21). If you are in Christ, then his relationship to you is an organic unity—as a head to a body. That means that his glory is your glory. "For you have died, and your life is hidden with Christ in God," the apostle Paul wrote. "When Christ who is your life appears, then you also will appear with him in glory" (Col. 3:3–4). His storyline is your storyline, and he is doing just fine.

If you are like me, this is often not enough. I may know, with my heart, that my glory is in Christ, that my future is secure in him, but it doesn't feel like it at the time. Sometimes when I am scared or doubting, I can feel as though God is, at best, far away, or, at worst, angry at me and punishing me with his absence. I am often frustrated that I cannot see my future clearly enough to relax in the providence of God. If that is you, you are hardly alone. And it is not because you live in a time now distant from the earthly ministry of Jesus. The disciples themselves, just before and just after seeing the transfigured glory of Jesus himself, while walking alongside him, couldn't see it either. In this time, the glory that we see is by faith, looking to Christ, no matter how we feel. It's when we embrace that the mystery of Christ is the defining factor of our lives that we actually can find meaning in them. And when we find meaning, we can endure anything.

Why can we not see it? The answer is partly because we could not understand it, were we to see anything other than a glimpse right now. "For I consider that the sufferings of this present time are not worth comparing with the glory that is to be revealed to us," the apostle Paul wrote. "For the creation waits with eager longing for the revealing of the sons of God," for the "freedom of the glory of the children of God" (Rom. 8:18–19, 21). Paul, like Jesus before him, used the metaphor of a universe in birth pangs, longing for this glory to be seen, for a new creation to be born (Rom. 8:22–23). You can no more really understand the glory of your future than you could explain to yourself as a baby in utero why the collapsing of what had always been home is actually good news.

Imagine trying to say to yourself being born what your life is like now, what life is like on this side of the uterine wall. The words would be gibberish, would not be understood, would probably sound just as scary as the cold air on the skin and the lights piercing the eyes feel. All you could do is stop explaining such things to yourself and just be there. You could hold that baby, and whisper in sing-song, "Everything is going to be all right; scream and fight all you need to, but you are loved and wanted, and everything is waiting for you." In a very real sense, except infinitely more so, that is exactly what God is doing for you right now. "So we do not lose heart. Though our outer self is wasting away, our inner self is being renewed day by day. For this light momentary affliction is preparing us for an eternal weight of glory beyond all comparison" (2 Cor. 4:16–17). This is beyond all comparison—we have no words to describe it. All we can do is wait with patience and with awe, finding meaning in the mystery of it all by seeing where the glory of God actually is: in the face of Jesus Christ. And we have seen that face.

The moment of Transfiguration was an unveiling of what is unseen at the present, and unveiling of what one day the entire cosmos will be like. The disciples must have wondered, "When will that cloud of glory come back?" But God would say to them, "He's right there in front of you—washing his beard out in that stream!" Jesus wasn't the means to the otherworldly light; the otherworldly light was about Jesus. If you want to know the end result of your life-story, to know how everything turns out, look no further than what God would unveil to John in what we call the Book of Revelation, about the transformed universe of the New Jerusalem. "And the city has no need of sun or moon to shine on it, for the glory of God gives it light and its lamp is the Lamb" (Rev. 21:23). Knowing then the name of Jesus, living as we do on the other side of his reign from heaven even as we wait for his reign everywhere else, we can say with even more confidence than David before us: "The LORD is my light and my salvation, whom shall I fear? The LORD is the stronghold of my life; of whom shall I be afraid?" (Ps. 27:1).

But even more than our lack of comprehension of unseen things is an even greater mystery still: that our individual life-plots are meant to join us to the life-plot of Jesus himself. We are decentered from our stories. We walk where he walked, and where he walked was to glory through cross-bearing. That's why Elijah's struggle to stand with courage is important for you. It's not so much that he is a model for you to follow as it is that he has gone where you too must go.

When Elijah stood on that mountain, convinced that all that awaited him was death, he could only hear a sound of inaudibility, a vibration of the thinnest silence. And the voice there seemed to be saying something more than, "What are you doing here, Elijah?" but he could not quite make it out. What Elijah heard in the wilderness by faith is the same voice you and I have heard as well, a Galilean accent saying, "Come, follow me." On the way down the mountain, the disciples of Jesus seemed impressed that they had seen Elijah, and were trying to fit his appearance into the future ordering of the kingdom. Jesus seemed to wave all that away, taking them once again to his walk toward the cross. Jesus seemed to be saying, "We are not waiting for Elijah; Elijah was waiting for us."

# Conclusion

Your life has meaning. Your life is a great mystery. And those are held together in Christ. Jesus is the plotline, and the story is good. You can have courage for the future because the future has a name, a face, and a blood type. You can embrace the Mystery, because the Mystery is alive and has plans for you. You need not peer into some future obituary for yourself, because you have already seen it. Above your head is a sign that reads "King of the Jews" and below your feet is a purple robe being gambled over by soldiers. That notice continues on through an emptied tomb and into realms you could not imagine right now.

Are there specifics of your story that you cannot know right now? Certainly. Is there anything so dramatically different from this that would make any difference to your future? No. "For I am sure that neither death nor life, nor angels nor rulers, nor things present nor things to come, nor powers, nor height nor depth, nor anything else in all creation, will be able to separate us from the love of God in Christ Jesus our Lord" (Rom. 8:38–39). And I don't know whether your obituary will end with an address for flowers to be sent, or a charity to which donations can be forwarded in your name. But I know that your real obituary—the real summation of your life—does not end with any of those things. Your real obituary ends with the words: "To be continued." It's not just that your life "turns out all right in the end," but that at the end of what you think is your life is when your life is just getting started.

As I finished writing this book, after everyone in my house had gone to bed, I stopped in the hallway and looked at that night light. I knelt down and noticed the craftsmanship of it, the wood carving of doors that can open and close. I noticed how the light framed everything there, and how the light was coming to me from the other side, just like it did when I was a suicidal teenager wondering if the universe was always winter and never Christmas, if there was a deeper magic than what I could sense around me. And I noticed that the figure of Lucy, as young and as scared as I was, is standing there, looking into what she cannot yet understand. She is scared but standing. And so am I. And so can you.

The lampposts that have helped us along this far can only point us beyond themselves to a greater Lampstand still. As I knelt there on the floor, what came to mind was a passage that

I would recite every week at the church where I preached, as a word of benediction. "In the beginning was the Word, and the Word was with God and the Word was God. He was in the beginning with God. All things were made through him, and without him was not anything made that was made. In him was life, and the life was the light of men. The light shines in the darkness, and the darkness has not overcome it. And the Word became flesh and dwelt among us, and we have seen his glory, glory as of the only Son from the Father, full of grace and truth" (John 1:1–5, 14). I read that passage every week because I believe it sums up the whole of the Bible. But, more than that, I read it because I needed to hear those words, out loud, every single week. My life depended on them. And still does.

I thought for a moment about the Light that has led me here, and will lead me home. I pondered what my fifteen-year-old self would think of my life now. What I would say to him, or to someone like him, if I were to see him. Then I wondered what my future self would say to me now, about all the things that rattle me and unsettle me, that fill me with cowardice even as I write about courage. And that made me think that I almost heard a voice somewhere in the thinnest silence, saying something like, "What are you doing here?" Or maybe it was a lion's roar. Either way, I just looked at the light from that lamppost for one more second, realizing that I do not know much about tomorrow, but I know everything I need to know about the Day after tomorrow.

And then I stood up.

Do not be afraid.

# Acknowledgments

This book would not be possible without the love and support of Maria, my wife of twenty-six years, and our five sons—Ben, Timothy, Samuel, Jonah, and Taylor. I am also grateful for my team at the Ethics and Religious Liberty Commission, especially Joshua Wester, Alex Ward, Daniel Patterson, Phillip Bethancourt (now pastor at Central Baptist Church in College Station, Texas), Brent Leatherwood, Travis Wussow, and Elizabeth Graham. I am also, as always, indebted to B&H Publisher Devin Maddox, my literary agent Andrew Wolgemuth, and the wise and skilled Jennifer Lyell. Moreover, as I have mentioned before, if it were not for friends such as David Prince, Andrew Peterson, Ben Shive, Ray Ortlund, Scott Patty, and others, I never would have written another word. That God has given me such people to love and to respect helps give me the courage to stand.

# Notes

## Chapter One

1. Laura Miller, *The Magician's Book: A Skeptic's Adventure in Narnia* (New York: Back Bay, 2009), 23.

2. Walker Percy, *Lost in the Cosmos: The Last Self-Help Book* (New York: Macmillan, 1983), 229.

3. James Baldwin, *The Fire Next Time* (New York: Delta, 1964), 30.

4. Ibid., 52–53.

5. Fyodor Dostoevsky, *The Brothers Karamazov,* trans. Richard Pevear and Larissa Volokhonsky (New York: Farrar, Straus, and Giroux, 2002), 362–63.

6. N. T. Wright, *Paul: A Biography* (New York: HarperOne, 2018), 64.

7. Mark Twain, "The Plutocracy," in *Mark Twain in Eruption: Hitherto Unpublished Pages About Men and Events by Mark Twain,* ed. Bernard DeVoto (New York: Harper & Brothers, 1922), 69.

8. Ibid., 70.

9. C. S. Lewis, *The Voyage of the Dawn Treader* (New York: HarperCollins, 1952), 247.

## Chapter Two

1. Art Spiegelman, "In the Dumps," *New Yorker*, 27 September 1993, 80–81.

2. David Quammen, *Monster of God: The Man-Eating Predator in the Jungles of History and the Mind* (New York: W.W. Norton, 2004).

3. David Whyte, *Consolations: The Solace, Nourishment, and Underlying Meaning of Everyday Words* (Langley, WA: Many Rivers Press, 2016), 42–43.

4. Josef Pieper, *The Four Cardinal Virtues: Prudence, Justice, Fortitude, Temperance* (South Bend: University of Notre Dame Press, 1966), 117.

5. Herman Bavinck, *Reformed Ethics*, vol. one, ed. John Bolt (Grand Rapids: Baker, 2019), 247.

6. Walker Percy, *The Moviegoer* (New York: Farrar, Straus & Giroux, 1960, 2019), 100.

7. Eugene Peterson, *When Kingfishers Catch Fire: A Conversation on the Ways of God Formed by the Words of God* (Colorado Springs: WaterBrook, 2017), 247–48.

8. J. R. R. Tolkien, *The Fellowship of the Ring* (Boston: Houghton Mifflin Harcourt, 1954), 83.

9. Flannery O'Connor, *Mystery and Manners: Occasional Prose*, ed. Sally and Robert Fitzgerald (New York: Farrar, Straus & Giroux, 1969), 118.

## Chapter Three

1. Seth Stephens-Davidowitz, *Everybody Lies: Big Data, New Data, and What the Internet Can Tell Us About Who We Really Are* (New York: HarperCollins, 2017).

2. Blaise Pascal, *Pensées*, trans. A. J. Kraislheimer (New York: Penguin, 1995), 37–43.

3. David Brooks, *The Road to Character* (New York: Random House, 2015).

4. Ziyad Marar, *The Happiness Paradox* (London: Reaktion, 2003), 32–33.

5. Ziyad Marar *Judged: The Value of Being Misunderstood* (London: Bloomsbury, 2018).

6. Seth Godin, *The Icarus Deception: How High Will You Fly?* (New York: Penguin, 2012), 124.

7. Seth Godin, *Linchpin: Are You Indispensable?* (New York: Penguin, 2010), 94.

8. Søren Kierkegaard, *Provocations: Spiritual Writings of Kierkegaard*, ed. Charles E. Moore (Walden, NY: Plough, 2002), 236.

## Chapter Four

1. Oliver Sacks, *Everything in Its Place: First Loves and Last Tales* (New York: Knopf, 2019), 140–43.

2. Ellen F. Davis, *Opening Israel's Scriptures* (New York: Oxford University Press, 2019), 209.

3. Ibid., 214.

4. Abraham Joshua Heschel, *I Asked for Wonder: A Spiritual Anthology*, ed. Samuel H. Dresner (New York: Crossroad, 1983), 104.

5. Stanley Milgram, *Obedience to Authority: An Experimental View* (New York: HarperCollins, 1974), 228.

6. Eitan Hersh, *Politics Is for Power: How to Move Beyond Political Hobbyism, Take Action, and Make Real Change* (New York: Scribner, 2020), 181.

7. Alan Moore and Dave Gibbons, *Watchmen* (New York: DC Comics, 1986–87).

8. Jason Lanier, *Ten Arguments for Deleting Your Social Media Accounts Right Now* (New York: Henry Holt & Co., 2018), 47–51.

9. Marilynne Robinson, *What Are We Doing Here?: Essays* (New York: Farrar, Straus and Giroux, 2018), 20.

10. Eudora Welty, "Must the Novelist Crusade?" in Eudora Welty, *On Writing* (New York: Modern Library, 2002), 82.

11. Ibid., 100.

12. Samuel L. Perry, *Addicted to Lust: Pornography in the Lives of Conservative Protestants* (New York: Oxford University Press, 2019).

13. Eugene Peterson, *As Kingfishers Catch Fire: A Conversation on the Ways of God Formed by the Words of God* (Colorado Springs: Waterbrook, 2017).

14. Vaclav Havel, "New Year's Address," in *Open Letters: Selected Prose, 1965–1990*, ed. Paul Wilson (London: Faber & Faber, 1991), 391.

15. Cass R. Sunstein, *Conformity: The Power of Social Influences* (New York: New York University Press, 2019), x.

16. Ibid.

17. Peter L. Berger, *The Noise of Solemn Assemblies: Christian Commitment and the Religious Establishment in America* (Garden City, NY: Doubleday, 1961), 85.

18. Ibid., 123.

19. Margaret J. Wheatley, *Who Do We Choose to Be? Facing Reality, Claiming Leadership, Restoring Sanity* (Oakland: Berrett-Koehler, 2017), 280.

20. William Bridges, *Transitions: Making Sense of Life's Changes*, second edition (New York: Perseus, 2004), 153–54.

21. Shirley Braverman and Joel Paris, "The Male Midlife Crisis in the Grown-up Resilient Child," *Psychotherapy* 30.4 (Winter 1993), 651–57.

## Chapter Five

1. Peter De Vries, *The Blood of the Lamb* (Chicago: University of Chicago Press, 1961, 2005), 96.

2. Max Oelschlaeger, *The Idea of Wilderness: From Prehistory to the Age of Ecology* (New Haven: Yale University Press, 1993), 42–43.

3. Jonathan Sacks, *Radical Then, Radical Now: On Being Jewish* (London: Bloomsbury, 2000), 84.

4. Robert Nisbet, *The Quest for Community: A Study in the Ethics of Order and Freedom* (San Francisco: Institute for Contemporary Studies, 1953, 1990), xxvi.

5. Peter Berger, *The Noise of Solemn Assemblies: Christian Commitment and the Religious Establishment in America* (New York: Doubleday, 1961), 131.

6. David Foster Wallace, *This Is Water: Some Thoughts, Delivered on a Significant Occasion, about Living a Compassionate Life* (New York: Little, Brown and Company, 2009), 109.

7. Dietrich Bonhoeffer, *Ethics* (New York: Simon & Schuster, 1995), 76–79

## Chapter Six

1. Bill Bishop, *The Big Sort: Why the Clustering of Like-Minded America Is Tearing Us Apart* (New York: Mariner, 2009).

2. Robert M. Sapolsky, *Behave: The Biology of Humans at Our Best and Worst* (New York: Penguin, 2017), 472–73.

3. Seth Godin, *We Are All Weird: The Rise of Tribes and the End of Normal* (New York: Penguin, 2011), 56.

4. C. S. Lewis, *The Weight of Glory and Other Addresses* (New York: HarperOne, 1949, 2001), 159.

5. Wendell Berry, *The Unsettling of America: Culture and Agriculture* (San Francisco: Sierra Club Books, 1997), 174.

6. Will Herberg, *Protestant, Catholic, Jew: An Essay in Religious Sociology* (Chicago: University of Chicago Press, 1955), 260–61.

7. Eun Lee, Fariba Karimi, Claudia Wagner, et al., "Homophily and Minority-Group Size Explain Perception Biases in Social Networks," *Nature Human Behavior* 3 (2019): 1078–87.

8. Peter L. Steinke, *Uproar: Calm Leadership in Anxious Times* (Lanham, MD: Rowman & Littlefield, 2019), 72.

9. Tom T. Hall, *The Storyteller's Nashville* (Spring House Press, Rev., Exp. ed., 2016), 146.

## Chapter Seven

1. Ian Johnson, *The Souls of China: The Return of Religion After Mao* (New York: Vintage, 2017), 27.

2. Henri Nouwen, *In the Name of Jesus: Reflections on Christian Leadership* (New York: Crossroad, 1992), 28–30.

3. Fyodor Dostoevsky, *The Brothers Karamazov*, trans. Richard Pevear and Larissa Volokhonsky (New York: Everyman's Library, 1992), 320–21.

## Chapter Eight

1. C. S. Lewis, *The Weight of Glory and Other Addresses* (New York: HarperCollins, 1949), 36.

2. Reynolds Price, *A Palpable God: Thirty Stories Translated from the Bible with an Essay on the Origins and Life of Narrative* (New York: Atheneum, 1978), 14.

3. Alasdair MacIntyre, *After Virtue: A Study in Moral Theory* (Notre Dame, IN: University of Notre Dame Press, 2007), 216.

4. Ibid., 217.

5. Frederick Buechner, *The Alphabet of Grace* (New York: HarperCollins, 1970, 1985), 51.

6. Ibid., 10.

7. E. M. Forster, *Aspects of the Novel* (New York: Harcourt, Brace & World, 1954), 86–94.

8. Christian Wiman, "The Cancer Chair," *Harper's Magazine,* February 2020, 56–57.

9. Leonard Cohen, "Anthem," Track 5 on *The Future*, Columbia, 1992.

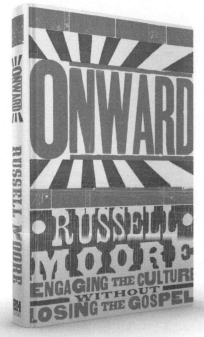